Physical Education Teachers on Physical Education

PHYSICAL EDUCATION TEACHERS ON PHYSICAL EDUCATION

A Sociological Study of Philosophies and Ideologies

Ken Green

Chester Academic Press

First published 2003
By Chester Academic Press
Learning Resources
Chester College of Higher Education
Parkgate Road
Chester CH1 4BJ

Printed and bound in the UK by the
Learning Resources Print Unit,
Chester College of Higher Education, Chester

Cover designed by the
Learning Resources Graphics Team

A catalogue record for this book
is available from the British Library

ISBN 1-902275-17-9

for Miranda

CONTENTS

Preface

The central themes of this book revolve around what have, for a number of years now, been of personal and professional interest to me: physical education (PE), philosophy and sociology. It is a book about the nature and purposes of PE; or, rather, the *supposed* nature and purposes of PE. Although based upon research conducted in the late 1990s, the issue at the heart of the book has its roots in my own experiences of PE — as both pupil and teacher. Similar to the "philosophies" of the teachers whose views interleave the pages of the book, my own perspective on PE has been inescapably intertwined with attachments to sport alongside recollections of PE as a pupil. As a student and teacher-trainee around the time when debate about PE took on a very public and political dimension, I was confronted by the prevailing philosophical view of education, and thus PE, as essentially academic.[1] And yet, it seemed readily apparent to me that PE in *practice* was quite removed from PE in *theory*: it was more about doing sport, about playing sport, than understanding sport — whatever that meant! It was this recognition and this involvement with the subject matter of PE that frequently led me into discussion with colleagues at a variety of secondary schools regarding their/our expectations of and for PE. What were PE teachers *thinking* about when they designed curricula? How did they *justify* what they were doing with children in the name of PE? The more I reflected on these issues, the more I noticed the hiatus between the philosophy of PE, as articulated by academic philosophers (and, albeit perhaps to a lesser extent, teacher-trainers), and PE as taught in a pragmatic and practically oriented way by PE teachers; an ostensible "gap" between theory and practice memorably caricatured in the portrayal of a PE teacher in the film *Kes*.

Little that I have witnessed in the name of PE, subsequently, led

---

[1] Academic in the sense of having to do with propositional knowledge; put colloquially, the kinds of knowledge that involve thinking rather than doing.

me to consider my initial impressions. Hence, the desire to explore PE teachers' views on teaching PE. Before doing so, however, I must acknowledge the teachers who gave of their time so freely and, in doing so, made the study possible. I would also like to thank Ivan Waddington, whose comments and advice permeate the whole project, and Peter Williams for bringing the project to fruition in the form of this book.

Abbreviations

AAHPERD	American Alliance for Health, Physical Education, Recreation and Dance
CCPR	Central Council for Physical Recreation
DCMS	Department for Culture, Media and Sport
DES	Department of Education and Science
DfEE	Department for Education and Employment
DNH	Department of National Heritage
GCSE	General Certificate of Secondary Education
HMI	Her Majesty's Inspectorate
HoD	head of department
HRE	health-related exercise
HRF	health-related fitness
ITT	initial teacher training
NCPE	National Curriculum for Physical Education
O&AA	outdoor and adventurous activities
OFSTED	Office for Standards in Education
ONS	Office for National Statistics
PE	physical education
PEA	Physical Education Association
PSE	personal and social education
PSHE	personal, social and health education
PTI	physical training instructor
QCA	Qualifications and Curriculum Authority
SCW	Sports Council for Wales
TGFU	teaching games for understanding
WO	The Welsh Office
WWI	World War I
WWII	World War II

1

Introduction

As the title suggests, this book explores physical education (PE) teachers' views on the subject they teach. More specifically, it presents an examination of what I will refer to as PE teachers' "philosophies";[1] that is to say, their views upon the nature and purposes of their subject. "Usually", according to Kirk (1990, p. 43), "debates over the content and teaching methods of physical education are contained within the profession". However, whilst it may be true to say that pedagogical matters continue — for the most part — to be conducted largely within the subject-community,[2]

[1] I have deliberately placed the word "philosophies" in quotation marks because my concern is, at least in part, with the relationship between, on the one hand, philosophies that have been articulated by academic philosophers seeking to define what they consider to be the "essential" characteristics or nature of PE and, on the other hand, ideas about PE that are held by teachers who have the practical task of teaching PE within schools. In strictly sociological terms, one might want to term these ideas "world-views" or "habituses" (van Krieken, 1998). However, for the following reasons, I have preferred to use the term "philosophies":

(i) in answer to questions in the study regarding their thoughts on what PE should be about, PE teachers themselves frequently referred to "my philosophy" in a manner that bore close resemblance to the aphoristic use of the term that has a common currency and which will be discussed in Chapter 2;

(ii) several authors in the broad field of the sociology of PE (see, for example, Armour, 1997; Armour and Jones, 1998; Evans, 1992) make use of the term "philosophy" when referring to teachers' ideas;

(iii) I am attempting to ascertain the "surface-level" or, as van Krieken (1998, p. 47) puts it, the "superficial portion" of their "consciousness" in the first instance; whilst,

(iv) reserving the more sociological concept of "habitus" for a more specific role in explaining PE teachers' "philosophies" in Chapter 5.

[2] The concept of subject- or policy-community is utilised to suggest that whilst PE teachers are a heterogenous, indeed somewhat disparate, group they nevertheless tend — along with other professional groups — to share at least one

content and "philosophies" are another matter. "In the latter half of the 1980s", Kirk (1990, p. 43) observed, PE programmes in British schools were "the subject of vociferous public debate". The relatively high public profile that PE attained in the 1980s has not diminished over the course of the last decade or so. In the early years of the twenty-first century, the supposed role(s) of school PE continues to excite considerable interest beyond the boundaries of the subject-community and, particularly, within government and media circles. For the most part, such interest has continued to revolve around the place of sport (and particularly "traditional" team games) in PE and the extent to which allegedly "progressive" PE teachers are deemed to have been guilty of "an insidious undermining of competitive sport in schools" (Kirk, 1990, p. 43).

It is perhaps not surprising that the nature and purposes of school PE are often a source of contestation between physical educationalists and other interested parties (such as Government, Sport England,[3] the media and sports' governing bodies), particularly in terms of how the latter perceive the proper aims of the former. What may seem more surprising is the variety and range of justifications for PE (for example, health promotion, character development, sporting excellence) within the subject-community itself. The history of PE has, in fact, been something of a history of struggle within the world of PE over particular definitions of what ought to count as PE (Evans, 1992; Kirk, 1992a, 1992b). As Kirk (1992b, p. 224) comments, since World War II, PE has been "a veritable battleground over attempts to define the subject...with the profession riven by acrimonious debate". The widespread media and political attention that PE has attracted in recent years has, unsurprisingly, been accompanied by warnings from academics that PE remained in need of a clear, consensual view of its nature and purposes — "a justification...to tell ourselves what we think we are about" (Parry, 1988, p. 108). There continued to be, or so it was

---

thing in common: concern with the professional and political standing of their subject. In this regard, they can be referred to as a subject- or policy-community insofar as, to paraphrase Houlihan (1991), they represent a group of professionals who display a significant concern for the maintenance and enhancement of their subject.

[3] Sport England is a quasi-autonomous non-governmental organisation (quango) with responsibility for sport.

claimed, a distinct lack of professional consensus about what being "physically educated" really meant or how being "physically educated" was best achieved (Alderson and Crutchley, 1990). "The notion of the physically educated person" remained, or so it was claimed, "vaguely defined" (Alderson and Crutchley, 1990, p. 40), whilst the "simple belief" persisted that involving children in a number of physical activities would lead to the achievement of "valuable educational ends" (p. 38). Notwithstanding the various "calls to arms", the search to establish a robust conceptualisation of PE has continued largely unattenuated (see, for example, Carr, 1997; McNamee, 1998; Parry, 1998; Reid, 1996a, 1996b, 1997).

Alderson and Crutchley (1990) were not alone among physical educationalists in hoping, even expecting, at the turn of the 1990s that the imminent arrival of the National Curriculum for Physical Education (NCPE) in 1992 would offer the PE profession "the opportunity…to make coherent statements about the nature of the subject and its concept of the physically educated person who should emerge from the curriculum" (p. 39).

It is interesting to note that the very existence of a perceived need to establish a consensual justification in order, as Parry (1988, p. 108) put it, "to defend and promote our subject", provided confirmation that PE had not achieved the kind of status and prominence in secondary-school curricula enjoyed by other, more established (and supposedly academic) subjects. Needless to say, as it turned out, even the emergence of the NCPE—with its lengthy explanatory outline of the nature of PE (see The Department of Education and Science/The Welsh Office [DES/WO], 1991) — failed to establish a definitive or consensual definition for PE. Nor did the official promise of a period of relative stability from further change (following the introduction of the revised NCPE in 1995) bring to an end debate about the nature and purposes of PE. If anything, NCPE (along with the subsequent revisions of 1995 and 2000) appears to have stimulated, rather than subdued, debate in some quarters, especially among academics in the subject-community (see, for example, Almond, 1996; Carr, 1997; Laker, 1996a, 1996b; Penney, Clarke and Kinchin, 2002; Reid, 1996a, 1996b, 1997).

Notwithstanding the two revised versions of NCPE (in 1995 and 2000), the supposedly "proper" aim or aims of PE evidently remain(s) a prominent issue at the level of academic theorising on the subject. In an often implicit, and occasionally explicit, form it is equally prominent at the level of PE teacher training and pedagogy (see, for example, Almond, 1996; Cale, 2000; Fisher, 1996; Fox, 1996; Penney and Harris, 1997). However, at the level of practice – that is to say, with the PE teacher him- or herself – it appears, anecdotally, that to the extent that teachers' concerns rise above the more pressing day-to-day matter of delivering their subject, their concerns have far less to do with philosophical debate regarding the role of PE than with the professional struggle for legitimacy, resources, power and status (Hardman, 1998).

Such apparent differences in orientation between those theorising and those practising PE make it clear that the nature and purposes of the subject are a legitimate area of interest for empirical socio-logical investigation as well as theoretical philosophical exploration. For, whilst sociologists cannot say what PE teachers *ought* to be thinking about their subject and doing in its name, they can seek to understand why they *think* what they think as well as *do* what they do. A sociological perspective can make sense of ideologies circu-lating within academic and professional debates, and the relation-ship between these and the "philosophies" (in the aphoristic sense) held by PE teachers. This is important for several reasons. Firstly, the absence of such an understanding will inevitably mean that PE teachers, teacher-trainers, academics, government ministers and other groups within what Houlihan (1991) refers to as the "policy community" of PE will be likely to "misunderstand" and, as a consequence, "talk past one another" (Wirth, 1960, p. xxvi). Secondly, the share of resources devoted to particular conceptions of PE will reflect the degree of power maintained by particular groups favouring particular conceptions.

Philosophical and Sociological Approaches to Conceptualising PE

At first glance, it appears something of a truism to suggest that establishing the aims and purposes of PE (as with education generally) is a *philosophical* matter. Educational rhetoric echoes a view that educational philosophers take to be more-or-less self-evident: namely that, "asking the right sort of conceptual questions about physical education" ought "to be seen as part of business as usual", not least because "in the context of teaching, a good professional is precisely one who continues to ask honest, intelligent and searching questions about the nature of his or her subject's contribution to general educational development" (Carr, 1997, p. 195). And yet, when viewed from a sociological standpoint, the very lack of a philosophical consensus regarding the nature and purposes of PE is illustrative of a *sociological* truism: that particular conceptions of PE can be identified as occupying the ideological high ground among the various groups that make up the subject-community at different times and in different places. Indeed, what constitutes a conception of PE is considerably more than a technical analysis of the terms *physical* and *education* as might be conducted by analytical philosophers. When investigated empirically, it seems likely that teachers' views on the nature and purposes of PE (as well as what PE looks like in practice) will have as much to do with their habituses[4] and their contexts—at the micro and macro levels—as any a priori intellectual reflection on the nature and purposes of their subject. Teachers' "philosophies" of PE, it seems clear, are *socially constructed*.

It is perhaps inevitable, then, that any attempt to make sense of teachers' views on PE cannot but incorporate a *sociological* appreciation of teachers "in the round"; for, as Wirth observes, perhaps "the most elemental and important facts" in making sense of PE teachers' perspectives upon PE "are those that are seldom debated and generally regarded as settled" (Wirth, 1960, p. xxiv); put another way: those that are "taken-for-granted".

O'Hear (1981, p. 1) alludes to the supposedly distinctive roles of philosophy and sociology when he suggests that a function of the former is "the systematic exposition and defence of the aims one thinks education ought to have, beyond any social functions it actually has or can be seen as having". The latter, for O'Hear, is the role of sociology. On this view, educational philosophy can be expected to focus upon the *aims*, rather than the *reality*, of PE. Whereas a philosophical perspective on the subject would be concerned with answering the question "What *should* PE be about?", the sociological perspective would concentrate upon what PE actually looks like in practice or, in effect, *is*. O'Hear's views

---

[4] What might be termed, after Elias (cited in van Krieken, 1998), the "second nature" of habitus as a concept, as well as its application, will be dealt with in greater detail in Chapter 2.

appear, then, to be representative of what might be broadly termed the philosophical perspective on education:

> One's philosophy of education, then, will be distinct from a sociology of education; reflecting one's values and concept of what men [*sic*] ought to be, as opposed to what they might [actually] be in any particular society. (O'Hear, 1981, p. 1)

On the face of it, sociology cannot tell us what to do but only what we actually do, in fact, do; it cannot tell us what we "ought" to think about PE but can only describe what we do think about PE. It is important to note, however, that whilst the contributions of philosophy and sociology appear quite distinctive, there is, nevertheless, a good deal of potential overlap. One might even say that there is (or at least needs to be) a degree of interdependence between the two approaches. Indeed, some (see, for example, Kilminster, 1998) would say that the development of the latter in recent years has made the former redundant! For the time being, however, we can be satisfied with Weber's (1949) observation that, whilst sociology might not be able to tell us what to do, it can tell us something about what it is possible to do. In this sense one might argue that all philosophy should be sociologically informed if it is to be concerned with realistic aims. Indeed, in outlining his intention to "show how people's general system of values and beliefs will affect what they think education should be" (1981, p. 3), O'Hear appears implicitly to acknowledge the inevitable (and, to some sociologists, quite proper) interrelationship between the two disciplines by encouraging an approach that might equally be characterised as sociological as (distinctly) philosophical. Yet, insofar as O'Hear merely relates thoughts to beliefs and values—that is to say, thoughts to thoughts, rather than thoughts to social circumstance and position—he fails to appreciate (or at least underplays) the importance of recognising and highlighting the links between ideas and social location.

O'Hear's implicit acknowledgement of the potentially intimate relationship between individuals' "philosophies" and ideology—as well as his explicit recognition of the significance of "extremely influential assumptions" (1981, p. 4)—points to one further sociological "truth": namely, the manner in which thoughts about education, and life generally, are in some way socially constructed. Arguably, it is the socially constructed nature of PE that almost inevitably dooms to failure attempts to establish, analytically, a consensual definition of the nature and purposes of PE. As Evans and Davies (1986, p. 15) point out, "What passes for physical education in the school curriculum is neither arbitrary nor immutable. It is a social and cultural construct, laden with *values that not all would adhere to or want to share*" (emphasis added). In other words, what we take for granted as PE is, in point of fact, a socio-historical construct: what PE teachers think and what they do is more-or-less constrained by what *has* been done and what *is* done in the name of PE by physical educationalists.

It is, therefore, a fundamental premise of this study that the various conceptions of the nature and purposes of PE are best understood in sociological rather than merely philosophical terms; that is to say, on the basis of an analysis of the relationships between "philosophies", ideologies and social location. It may be useful to underscore this point by adapting the observation of Freidson (1983; cited in Macdonald, 1995) on the process of professionalisation: one is not attempting to determine what PE is about in an absolute sense so much as how physical educationalists arrive at a preferred conception of the subject by their activities. From this perspective, the kinds of ideal-type constructions frequently found in analytical philosophy of education are of limited value. Whilst they tell us what a given social grouping might want or expect PE to become, they do not tell us what physical educationalists themselves think they are about in the process of teaching PE. An appreciation of the ideologies underlying PE teachers' "philosophies" (as they articulate them), in conjunction with their perceptions of the situations they find themselves in, may help us to appreciate better the "nature" of contemporary PE.

This notwithstanding, before pressing on it is worth reminding ourselves that it would be a mistake simply to assume that an insider's perspective is, of necessity, a more accurate and, therefore, more adequate perspective on a topic such as PE. Individuals' perceptions always require contextualising; they require locating in a broader framework. Consequently, this book will attempt to establish how other facets of PE teachers' situations, such as pressures of a professional kind and political developments, for example, interact with prior beliefs and training to influence their "philosophies" of PE. And, indeed, why teachers in different work situations (for example, senior or junior members of staff — such as heads of department — and men or women) may well hold views of PE that differ, sometimes fundamentally, from one another.

The sociological approach adopted in this study is rooted in figurational sociology (see Chapter 2). This approach requires that teachers' "philosophies" be set in their overall context — their configuration — rather than resorting to a convenient caricature of reality by focusing upon the impact of any particular variable (for example, academic philosophy, the impact of NCPE or even individual teachers' personalities) on behaviour — as if a direct causal relationship could be established between the existence of a variable, such as a particular political policy, and the prevalence of a particular "philosophy" of PE. A sociological — and specifically figurational approach — is particularly useful in this regard inasmuch as it encourages us to think not in terms of single causes but rather in terms of multi-causality: causes as aspects of more complex developmental processes. Indeed, we can go one step further, by appreciating that teachers' "philosophies" and the ideologies that underpin them are not so much caused by the social situation but, rather, they constitute an aspect of those situations.

In short, the book will attempt to throw sociological light on the extent to which, as well as the manner in which, the everyday "philosophies" of PE teachers are underpinned by particular ideologies (for example, of health and sport): belief systems that are, in turn, a reflection of wider ideological, economic and cultural forces. It is intended to use teachers' "philosophies" as a basis for an understanding of how and why particular views come to dominate the ideological high ground of PE. The upshot should then be a clear portrayal of the processes at work in the development of particular "philosophies" among teachers of PE.

All told, the book will attempt to demonstrate the benefits of a sociological approach to an ostensibly philosophical issue by making much more complex — but also much more adequate — our understanding of the social roots of prevailing conceptualisations of PE "philosophies". The book will attempt to reveal the ways in which influential ideologies are, in the words of Kirk (1992b, p. 226) "constructed by people interacting at particular times, in specific locations, in response to their immediate circumstances, and infused with their interests, preoccupations and values". In addition, it will attempt to tease out the manner in which the ideologies underpinning teachers' "philosophies" are impacted upon by the constraints of everyday practice in terms of teachers' working situations; that is to say, the extent to which "philosophies" are "part and parcel" of teachers' ordinary, everyday working lives.

Chapter 2—"A Sociological Perspective on Physical Education Teachers' 'Philosophies'"—provides both an outline of the nature of sociological approaches to topics such as PE and a justification for the particular sociological perspective adopted in the book—that of figurational sociology. In addition, it will point up the way in which a sociological approach to knowledge and beliefs helps us to make adequate sense of why PE teachers' thoughts and practices are as they are.

Focusing upon "Ideological Themes in Physical Education", Chapter 3 will bring the ideologies that underpin contemporary academic justifications for PE to the surface. In the process, it will compare and contrast the fortunes of what is characterised as the pre-eminent traditional "philosophy" of PE (with its emphasis on sport and particularly team games) with the ideology that is seen as having risen to a prominent position on the ideological high ground of the subject-community through the 1980s and into the early part of the 1990s: that of health.

Chapter 4, entitled "Physical Education Teachers on Physical Education", lies at the heart of the book and revolves around a study of several dozen teachers from the north-west of England in 1998. The chapter provides an outline of PE teachers' "philosophies" of PE and, in the process, identifies those ideological themes that are more-or-less prominent within PE teachers' views on their subject.

Chapter 5 will conceptualise the everyday "philosophies" of PE teachers not so much in terms of the reflections of the gladiatorial combat between the supposedly "grand (academic) philosophies" of education as such, but rather—and, arguably, more adequately—as the outcome of a complex interweaving of a network of relationships at both micro and macro levels. This will necessitate identification of processes internal and external to PE that inevitably provide the context in which and to which teachers respond. Thus, by way of explaining how PE teachers have arrived at their everyday "philosophies", the chapter will explore PE teachers' figurations at the personal, local and national levels. At the personal level, the processes will include the sporting and career biographies that help form teachers' habituses. At the local level, they will incorporate institutional relationships and expectations, as well as the practical day-to-day issues circumscribing teachers' thoughts and deeds. At the national level, the constraints of national legislation and policy as well as various broader social processes (such as the medicalisation of life and the professionalisation of work) are identified as the bases of ideological division among influential groups (for example, academics in the PE subject-community and the Government).

In essence, the body of the book has two phases: a descriptive phase (Chapters 3 and 4) and an explanatory phase (Chapters 2 and 5). The concluding chapter, Chapter 6, will offer a summary of the "philosophies" of PE teachers, explaining these in terms of figurational sociology and identifying connections with a sociological understanding of knowledge. In the light of the two phases identified above, it is worth making one final observation about the structure of the book. Those readers more interested in what PE teachers have to say about their subject than adopting a sociological perspective as such might want to "skip" straight from the Introduction to Chapters 3 and 4. In order to make sense of Chapter 5, however, it would then be a good idea to return to Chapter 2 prior to "Making Sense of Physical Education Teachers' 'Philosophies'".

The Study upon which the Book is Based

The study (Green, 2000) around which the book revolves investigated PE teachers' "philosophies" from a sociological perspective. It was based upon semi-structured interviews conducted with 35 PE teachers from 17 schools in the north-west of England in late June/early July of the 1998 summer term. The sampling frame for the study was all male and female PE teachers at 25 secondary schools in the state education system in two unitary authorities (formerly one county council). A purposive sampling method – a non-probability method and one commonly employed in qualitative research (Bowling, 1997) – was utilised. This form of sample selection is used to identify particular people or groups of people –

in this case, PE teachers — who are broadly known to the researcher and with a specific purpose in mind. That purpose "reflects the particular qualities of the people...chosen and their relevance to the topic of the investigation" (Denscombe, 1998, p. 15). In this vein, the various schools, and PE departments therein, were chosen to represent the city, new towns and rural locations typical of the region. In that respect the area was not atypical of non-metropolitan areas in the UK with a variety of urban, suburban and rural communities as well as a broad economic base, albeit with a relatively small ethnic-minority population. This purposive sampling frame resulted in a sample that was, in one sense, a convenience sample, insofar as it was constituted of PE teachers at those schools — located variously in a small city, two towns and several villages — that were "first to hand", as Denscombe (1998, p. 16) puts it. Consequently, the resultant sample consisted of those teachers who responded to the first round of interview requests.

In many ways this configuration of purposive and convenience sampling threw up what — in the absence of available official data — might be plausibly regarded as a suitable cross-section of PE teachers for the purposes of the study. The sample consisted of 15 male and 20 female teachers from 17 schools of which 15 (8 male/7 female) were heads of department (HoDs) and 20 (7 male/13 female) were main grade teachers of PE. Thirteen of the teachers (of whom three were HoDs) were 30 years of age or younger. Six (two HoDs) were between 31 and 40. Fifteen were between 41 and 50 years (9 HoDs) and one (HoD) was over 50.

Qualitative approaches, such as the one employed in the study, typically involve an attempt to identify the central features of, and patterns within, interviewees' responses via a categorisation of content. Content analysis is the relatively detached and systematic deconstruction of texts, whether in the form of the printed or spoken word. Texts can be interpreted on a number of levels, but an overriding concern is the attempt to comprehend the perspective of the interviewee. Thus, the interview data from the study were arranged into what might be termed "common clusters" or "categories of meaning" based upon the core themes of the interviews. Among the broad areas of enquiry that provided the structure for the interviews were teachers' views regarding what PE should be about, the relationship between teachers' "philosophies" and their professed practice, and their perceptions of context. The data were broken down into units for analysis via the continual and ongoing revisiting of interview transcriptions and field notes in order to refine the categories of meaning subsequently employed to explain the data. Thus, the original categories were amended to incorporate areas of concern or interest that emerged during the interviews.

2

A Sociological Perspective on
Physical Education Teachers' "Philosophies"

In this chapter, I intend to clarify what is meant by a sociological perspective as well as which particular sociological perspective I have chosen to adopt and why. This will be followed by a brief résumé of the particular ways in which the two concepts central to the book — philosophy and ideology — will be employed. It should be noted that the nature of a book such as this means that only a flavour of the two main themes of the chapter — (figurational) sociology and the sociology of knowledge — can be provided. Readers interested in exploring each theme in greater depth are directed to the work of Abram de Swaan (2001), Robert van Krieken (1998), Stephen Mennell and Johan Goudsblom (1998) and Richard Kilminster (1998).[1]

Simply put, sociology involves the study of people in society and the groups and patterns their interactions form. In this sense, sociology is about people in the plural: pluralities of people "interdependent with each other in a variety of ways" (Mennell and Goudsblom, 1998, p. 39). Such interdependence is a consequence of the fact that people are inevitably and always dependent upon and

---

[1] Abram de Swaan's *Human Societies: An Introduction* is a delightfully readable introduction to sociology with more than a hint of figurational sociology visible just below the surface. Robert van Krieken's *Norbert Elias* is part of Routledge's Key Sociologists series and is the ideal introduction to the work of Elias as the founding father of figurational sociology. Stephen Mennell and Johan Goudsblom's book entitled *Norbert Elias: On Civilization, Power and Knowledge* offers a more detailed study of Elias's work incorporating sections of his most important works, particularly related to the sociology of knowledge. Richard Kilminster's *The Sociological Revolution* offers a more detailed (figurational) sociological perspective on the relationship between sociology and philosophy and quite provocatively suggests that the development of the former has made much, if not all, of the latter redundant!

depended on by others — head teachers and pupils, for example, in the case of PE teachers. Adopting a sociological perspective involves appreciating the consequences of such interdependence: that is to say, the ways in which people's lives — both personal and professional — are lived within and, consequently, are shaped by the networks (or figurations) they form together. In what follows I intend to elaborate upon those aspects of these networks or figurations, and of figurational sociology itself, that are particularly germane to the theme of this book.

A Figurational Sociological Perspective

In the eyes of a number of sociologists, figurational sociology is firmly rooted in the tradition of mainstream (Weberian) British sociology, with its apparent emphasis upon multiple sites of power. Regardless of the veracity of this claim, the overarching reasons for adopting a figurational sociological approach in this book are broadly twofold: firstly, what I take to be the manner in which figurational sociology serves as a synthesis and refinement of several prominent branches of classical and contemporary sociology (van Krieken, 1998); and secondly, the manner in which, to my mind, figurational sociology offers a more satisfactory resolution of some of the central issues of sociology, most notable among which is the thorny issue of structure–agency dualism or, put another way, the nature of the relationship between people and society. I will deal with this issue first.

People and Society

One of the main objects of sociology is to "enlarge our understanding of human and social processes and to acquire a growing fund of more reliable knowledge about them" (Elias, 1978, p. 17). For all sociologists, in order to do this one is bound to confront the very way in which sociologists conceptualise people in society. And it is with foundational issues such as this that sociology comes face to face with its most profound hurdle. It is the nature of the relationship between people and the society they form (whilst being a part thereof) that confounds and perplexes many students of the discipline. Indeed, it is in relation to this fundamental issue that, arguably, the distinctive approach of figurational sociology offers a ground-breaking perspective on an enduring problem.

For a large number of sociologists it has been, and continues to be, conventional to conceptualise society *sui generis*; that is to say, as an object that exists in its own right (Frisby and Sayer, 1986). The associated distinction between society (the "structure") and the individual (the "agent") continues to represent something of an orthodoxy in much sociological writing. Such a dichotomous distinction, it is suggested, remains a fundamental hindrance to the development of a more adequate "science" of society. Consequently, the problem of adequately conceptualising the relationship between people and the societies they form has remained a thorn in the side of sociological theory, despite various high-profile attempts to resolve the issue (see, for example, Giddens, 1984). For figurationalists the root cause of this persistent problem lies in the conventional conceptualisation of individual and society as distinct entities. For those favouring what is traditionally termed a "structuralist" conception of individuals in society, people appear at the mercy of more-or-less (and usually more) deterministic "forces". Society, on this view, exists *sui generis* and, as such, exerts pressures on people to think and act in particular ways—ways that reflect and are dependent upon the individual's position or positions in the social structure. However, although under certain conditions (for example, as a newly qualified PE teacher), people feel themselves to be subject to "compelling forces" (Elias, 1978) — and thus perceive society to exist in its own right — there is an important distinction to be made between *feeling compelled* and *being bound*. For figurationalists this is the nub of the dilemma. What might appear conceptual nit-picking is, in fact, fundamental to the sociological enterprise inasmuch as everything else is contingent upon a notion of people and society that represents a more adequate conceptualization than the orthodox dichotomy. Consequently, at the heart of the (figurational) sociological perspective adopted in this book is the premise that, whilst they may nevertheless be experienced as external, "social forces are in fact forces exerted by people over one another and over themselves" (Elias, 1978, p. 17). For figurationalists, the portrayal of human beings as "self-contained" and thus "separate" individuals impacted upon by a social structure that is theorised as distinct from (almost "above" and "beyond") those "individuals" distorts the sociological perspective from the outset. In this regard, Elias

(1978, p. 72) comments:

> the figurations of interdependent human beings cannot be explained if one studies human beings singly. In many cases the opposite procedure is advisable—one can understand many aspects of the behaviour or actions of individual people only if one sets out from the study of the pattern of their interdependence, the structure of their societies, in short from the figurations they form with each other.

Traditionally, for sociologists, the relationship between the individual and society is an a priori matter. For Elias, what encouraged sociologists to conceptualise the issue thus was what people actually saw or observed; that is to say, what was observed were individuals in groups. Hence the common-sense tendency towards conceptualising people as both distinct from and, at the same time, a part of society. What marks figurational sociology out is the distinctly Eliasian understanding of that relationship. Thus, the cornerstone of a figurational approach is the conceptualization of society as interdependent people *in the plural* and individuals as interdependent people *in the singular*; as Murphy, Sheard and Waddington (2000) put it, sociology is concerned not with *homo clausus* but with *homines aperti*, with "people bonded together in dynamic constellations". In this manner, the figurational perspective offers a conceptualisation of the relationship between people and society which "neither metaphysically postulates the existence in societies of supraindividual structures that are 'real', nor sees societies simply as aggregates of detached and independent individuals" (Dunning, 1999, p. 19).

This brings me to the central organizing concept of figurational sociology—the concept of "figuration" itself (Murphy *et al.*, 2000)—that marks such a perspective out as a potentially more productive way of making sense of people and their networks (for example PE teachers in schools).

Figurations
A central feature of figurational sociology is the assumption that people and their activities are best viewed in terms of the *networks* of social relationships of which they are always and inevitably a part. Thus, for all sociologists, a key task of sociology is to "shed light onto the structure and dynamics" of these networks and the

various bonds or "chains of interdependency" (Dunning, 1996, p. 203) linking people to each other. Conceptualised in this way, people are seen to be related to (or interdependent with) a large number, and wide range, of other people at one and the same time. As Mennell and Goudsblom (1998, p. 22) observe, "In order to understand the feelings, thoughts, and action of any group of people, we have always to consider the many social needs by which these people are bonded to each other and to other people." These bonds form "composite units" (Mennell and Goudsblom, 1998, p. 114) or groups of people with a particular structure and particular network of relationships. Interdependency becomes an increasingly useful way of conceptualising relationships as the networks people are involved in grow and become ever more complex (for example, between PE teachers and their department heads, senior management, local sports clubs and governing bodies of sport). Mennell and Goudsblom (1998, p. 18) put it like this:

> as webs of interdependence spread, more people become more involved in more complex and more impenetrable relations. Less abstractly: more people are forced more often to pay more attention to more people, in more varying circumstances. This produces pressures towards greater consideration of the consequences of one's own action for other people on whom one is in one way or another dependent.

It is important to note, however, that the relationships of which figurationalists speak are not necessarily, nor predominantly, relationships of the "face-to-face" variety. Rather, networks (or figurations) are constituted in the inevitable interconnectedness of interdependent people in the plural and incorporate people (individually and in groups) and processes (such as the academicisation of PE [Green, 2001; Reid, 1996a]) — past or present, recognised or unrecognised. In sum, for figurationalists, the character of social life can only be understood if people are "conceptualised as *interdependent...*comprising *figurations* and characterised by socially and historically specific forms of *habitus*, or personality structure" (van Krieken, 1998, p. 55; emphases in the original). In the context of the overarching theme of the book, it is worth saying a little more about habitus as a dimension of figurations.

Habitus

For figurationalists, people are always and everywhere interdependent with other people and groups of people — via webs of social relationships or figurations. Within these various figurations the personality make-up or "habitus" of people develops. Citing Camic (1986), van Krieken (1998, p. 47) suggests that the concept of habit or habitus refers to:

> the durable and generalized disposition that suffuses a person's action throughout an entire domain of life or, in the extreme instance, throughout all of life — in which case the term comes to mean the whole manner, turn, cast, or mold of the personality.

This "second nature", or "automatic, blindly functioning apparatus of self-control", as Elias (cited in van Krieken, 1998, p. 59) referred to habitus, has several interrelated features worthy of note. The organisation of one's psychological make-up into a habitus is, according to van Krieken (1998, pp. 59-60), "a continuous *process* which (begins) at birth and continue(s) throughout a person's childhood and youth" (emphasis in the original). Whilst habitus develops most rapidly and tends to have greatest impact during this "more impressionable phase" — namely, "during childhood and youth" (p. 59) — it, nevertheless, continues to develop throughout a person's life. Finally, "the ways in which the formation of habitus (changes) over time...(can) only be properly understood in connection with changes in the surrounding social relations" (p. 60).

It is worth elaborating upon this final point. Whilst habitus forms and develops as an aspect of social interdependencies — and has a tendency to vary as the social structure varies — it is noteworthy that habitus might change at a slower rate than the surrounding social relations (van Krieken, 1998). Hence, it is frequently the case that people's outlook on life (such as PE teachers' views on the nature and purposes of their subject) remains to a greater or lesser extent tied to "yesterday's social reality" (for example, PE as practised prior to the introduction of the National Curriculum for Physical Education in 1992), as van Krieken (1998, p. 61) puts it. Notwithstanding this observation, it is worth reiterating the point that, whilst habitus is substantially formed during early life, it remains open to development as the interdependent networks people are involved in become more-or-less complex and more-or-less compelling. The opaqueness of their figurations to those involved makes "game models" a complementary concept to that of interdependency.

Game Models

For figurational sociologists, conceptualising teachers' networks of interdependencies in terms of a multi-level game holds out the promise of a more adequate conception of the manner in which the complexities of teachers' circumstances impact upon their thoughts and practices. For Elias, game models utilise "the image of people playing a game as a metaphor for people forming societies together" and, in doing so, "serve to make certain problems about social life more accessible to scientific reflection" (Elias, 1978, p. 92). In particular, game models bring out particularly clearly the ways in which interdependencies inescapably constrain people to a greater or lesser extent. This is held to occur in a manner analogous to that in which, in a game, the dependency of a player on the intentions and actions of team-mates and opponents inevitably influences the player's own intentions and actions. Games vary with regard to the number of players in the game and the number of levels or tiers on which the game is played; as the number of players and the complexity of the game increase, so it becomes increasingly difficult for those involved in the game to frame "a mental picture of the course of the game and its figuration" (Elias, 1978, p. 84). The absence of an overall mental picture of the game of which he or she is a part may result, in turn, in the player becoming disoriented. The upshot can be that the game appears, to those involved, to take on a life of its own. The potential significance of developments of this sort becomes apparent when Elias (1978, p. 94) observes that, "…being interdependent with so many people will very probably compel individual people to act in a way they would not act except under compulsion". In this manner, game models of social interdependency have the potential to "show how the web of human relations changes when the distribution of power changes" (Elias, 1978, p. 80), as well as how power-ratios influence the extent to which the moves of one person or group can influence, if not determine, the moves of another, as well as the final outcome. Thus, from a figurational perspective, processes such as education can usefully be conceptualised as multi-player, multi-tier games. The analogy of multi-tier, multidimensional games for the workings of social processes enables one to focus on a particularly important aspect of processes such as education: namely, the existence of "bonds" between people who ostensibly see themselves as belonging to one side or another (for example, PE teachers, head teachers, sports development officers and sports coaches).

Power and Power-Ratios

Conceptualising social processes in terms of the model of a game brings to the fore the centrality of power and "the polymorphous nature of sources of power" (Elias, 1978, p. 92). Mennell and Goudsblom (1998, p. 36) describe the phenomenon thus:

> Throughout life, we depend on others for things we need, want, or value; and others are dependent upon us for the things they need. This simple fact means that power-ratios are a feature of all human relationships.

Power is, therefore, a central dimension of interdependencies, and the many kinds of figurations or webs of interdependency of which people are a part are characterised by many different sorts of balances of power (Elias, 1978). Whilst interdependencies are "reciprocal", they are also typically unequal (Mennell and Goudsblom, 1998, p. 22): "usually one party in a social relationship tends, at least in certain respects, to be more dependent than the other party" (for example, head teachers, heads of department and teachers) with the result that an uneven balance of power—or "power-ratio" —exists "that directly affects the way both parties act and feel towards each other" (Mennell and Goudsblom, 1998, p. 22). It is important to note that power here is conceptualised as a process rather than as something static. For figurationalists, "the more relatively equal become the power-ratios among large numbers of people and groups" the more likely it is that the outcome — of either thought or action — "will be something that no single person or group has planned or anticipated" (Mennell and Goudsblom, 1998, p. 23). Hence, the likelihood that "yesterday's unintended social actions" will become "today's unintended social conditions of intended human actions" (p. 23). The structured processes that can be identified as a result of this, whilst not having lives of their own, "are then experienced as compelling processes by the people caught up in them" (p. 23). Having said this, it is important to recognise that power relations are internally dynamic because power balances, like human relationships per se, "are bi-polar at least, and usually multi-polar" (Elias, 1978, p. 74). Thus, any tendency towards conceptualising the power struggles that groups of people find themselves involved in as broadly uni-dimensional should be resisted. For figurationalists, the lengthening chains of interdependence in modern societies have resulted in a reduction of the power differentials between people and groups of people.

The first part of this chapter has provided a thumbnail sketch of some concepts central to figurational sociology and the sociological perspective adopted in the book. In what follows, I intend to outline the implications of a figurational perspective for a study of this kind; that is to say, a sociological study of what people know or, rather, claim to know — in other words, the sociology of knowledge.

The Sociology of Knowledge

The study of human knowledge is characterised by two main traditions (Wilterdink, 1977; Elias, 1978). On the one hand, there is a philosophical tradition — which Elias (1978) refers to as a classical theory of knowledge — that centres conceptually upon the notion of "a solitary individual" who "thinks, perceives, and performs" in isolation. On such a view, "knowledge is seen as independent of social processes" whilst "definite and certain knowledge" is seen as "the ideal which can be attained by following certain rules of rationality" (Elias, 1978, p. 37). On the other hand, there stands a sociological tradition wherein, "all knowledge is regarded as culture-bound, socially determined, and therefore ideological" (Wilterdink, 1977, p. 110). For Elias, such views can be seen to represent a false dichotomy, "in which knowledge can only be true or arbitrary" (Wilterdink, 1977, p. 111). From a (figurational) socio-logical perspective, however, it is more accurate as well as more productive to view knowledge as lying along a continuum ranging from *involvement* to *detachment*; a concept that represents "marginal poles between which people's thoughts and actions are normally steered" (Murphy *et al.*, 2000) both by themselves and others.

A figurational sociology of knowledge utilises the concept of involvement-detachment in order to build a more properly socio-logical appreciation of what we refer to as "knowledge". It is worth saying a little more at this juncture about involvement-detachment.

The concept of involvement-detachment emerged as one of the main features of Norbert Elias's seminal work on the sociology of knowledge. For Elias and figurationalists, "a balance of emotional involvement and detachment is present in virtually all human behaviour" (Murphy *et al.*, 2000, p. 94). Thus, to understand why people think and act as they do one needs to appreciate that thought and behaviour tend to reflect the impact of emotion as well as reason. Indeed, people's passions frequently impact more substantially on their thoughts and behaviours than abstract reasoning and reflection. Conceptualising thinking in terms of degrees of involvement and detachment (Murphy *et al.*, 2000), it is claimed, holds out the promise of a more adequate conception of knowledge than the more conventional dichotomy of objectivity and subjectivity wherein things are either factual or arbitrary and personal.

With the concept of involvement-detachment in mind it is worthwhile reminding ourselves of two related points. Firstly, that the sociology of knowledge is not concerned with abstract ideas as such. It does not set out to "criticize thought on the level of the assertions themselves" (Mannheim, 1960, p. 238); that is to say, the coherence of the ideas themselves. Secondly, knowledge and ideas should not be seen as the products of an individual's thinking (Mennell and Goudsblom, 1998). Consequently, because of its centrality to an adequate appreciation of the *social* nature of knowledge, sociology teases out the inevitably human dimension of knowledge on the premise that "a large part of thinking...cannot be correctly understood, as long as its connection with the existence of the social implications of human life are not taken into account" (Mennell and Goudsblom, 1998, p. 241) – hence, the significance for figurational sociology of the concept of involvement-detachment in an appreciation of the social "nature" of knowledge. As Outhwaite (1983, p. 185; summarising Scheler, 1924) puts it: "systems of ideas have an internal logic of their own, but...'real factors' in the outside world determine the rate of development and the influence of these ideas". Outhwaite's philosophical perspective requires qualification in order to underline the figurational point that not only the "rate" and "influence", but more fundamentally the *generation* of these ideas is intimately related to the "real factors in the outside world". Indeed, it requires additional qualification insofar as it is more accurate to conceptualise ideas as an *aspect* of the "real world" rather than separate from it. Of particular interest to the sociologist are, then, the "existential factors" (Mannheim, 1960, p. 240) associated with "the social position of the assertor" (p. 255). For figurationalists, the intellectual sphere is part of the social process, and any attempt to separate the former from the latter threatens to perpetuate a false dichotomy.

A sociology of knowledge is, therefore, concerned primarily with the "situational relativity" of knowledge (Mannheim, 1960, p. 244). It is worth reiterating the point, however, that an account of the social construction of knowledge is not preferred to, or intended to replace, a philosophical approach, which raises different but equally legitimate problems. Neither, for that matter, does a sociologically informed epistemology invalidate particular justificatory arguments for particular "truths" — that is to say, their validity. Rather, the claim is that knowledge, "besides being a proper subject matter for logic and psychology, becomes fully comprehensible only if it is viewed sociologically" (Wirth, 1960, p. xxvii). Nonetheless, whilst for Mannheim (1960, p. 258) "the nature of the genesis of an assertion may become relevant to its truth", it may be more accurate to suggest that, whilst the genesis of an assertion may not be germane to its truth value per se, it will help us understand why particular people in particular circumstances *believe* it to be true.

The Application of a Figurational Sociology of Knowledge to PE

It is apparent that, from the perspective of figurational sociology, PE teachers' everyday "philosophies" cannot be satisfactorily *understood* in terms of purely intellectual or technical processes. Put another way, PE teachers' views of their subject cannot be adequately explained in a context that attempts to detach the ideas from the people or groups holding them. In contrast to the largely (if not entirely) technical or "analytical" approach to ideas associated with PE philosophy since the 1970s, for sociologists conceptions of PE inevitably reflect "the penetration of the social process into the intellectual sphere" (Mannheim, 1960, p. 240) at the differing levels of the teachers' figurations or networks of interdependence. PE teachers' views inevitably bear witness to what *has* happened at a personal level (for example, in their lives and career thus far) as well as what *is* happening at the local (for example, the school) and national (for example, governmental) levels. Hence, the sociology of knowledge is, according to Mannheim (1960), "an *empirical* theory of the actual relations of knowledge to the social situation" (p. 257; emphasis added); that is to say, an investigation of the relationship between what is claimed and the *circumstances* of the claimer.

Thus, it is argued, the ways PE teachers view their subject and their work as teachers can only be adequately understood if one contextualises their views within their particular configuration of experiences and relationships – at what will be termed the personal, local and national levels – whilst, at the same time, locating these within wider social processes such as professionalisation, sportisation and medicalisation. As practitioners, PE teachers are no more likely than any other teacher or "professional" person, for that matter, to engage in, as Waddington (1975, p. 48) puts it, "the consideration of abstract philosophical principles". Insofar as PE teachers consider the nature and purposes of PE, their concern is likely to arise from, and be shaped by, their predispositions in association with the day-to-day practice of their profession, such as writing curricula, justifying aims and objectives to colleagues, external agencies and so forth. It may well be their orientation to the mundanities of their "practical" positions as much as, if not more than, their perspective on any "theoretical" positions on the nature and purposes of PE (as outlined either by government publications or educational philosophers) that has the more significant impact on PE teachers' views of their subject.

The interdependencies that are a feature of teachers' figurations take a variety of forms. Some interdependencies – for example, between PE teachers and their departmental and school colleagues or, for that matter, the children in their charge – are easily identifiable. More opaque, but potentially every bit as significant for teachers' thoughts and actions, are the ties that bind PE teachers to parents, government departments, professional bodies, head teachers and so forth. The bonds between PE teachers and those near or far, so to speak, who form their figurations both enable and constrain (Murphy *et al.*, 2000); that is to say, the relationships between a teacher and other teachers, parents, pupils or other groups of teachers or educationalists, for example, may encourage or inhibit the development of particular views or practices, directly or indirectly.

PE teachers are, of necessity, frequently to be found in a variety of composite units including departments, professional bodies and sporting communities. This is a significant point. In making sense of the "philosophies" of teachers and the penetration of particular ideologies into their thoughts upon the nature and purposes of PE, it is crucial to recognise the centrality of the interdependency of people to the process of thinking. Interdependency is a pivotal concept in figurational sociology, and making sense of the network of interdependencies in which people such as PE teachers are involved helps one appreciate the centrality of power in these networks. Of particular pertinence to this study is Mennell and Goudsblom's (1998, p. 125) observation that there is "a limit to the span of the web of interdependence within which an individual can orientate himself (*sic*) suitably and plan his personal strategy over a series of moves". PE teachers are compelled to orientate themselves outwith as well as within the secondary-school setting. As parents, for example, become increasingly powerful and influential, it becomes correspondingly difficult for teachers to resist their claims for information about, and involvement in, their children's education, even if they are inclined to do so. Thus teachers' ideas as well as their practices can only be adequately explained when one takes into account the "compelling forces" (Mennell and Goudsblom, 1998, p. 118) and power-ratios impacting upon them through the interdependencies in which they are inescapably involved — interdependencies with not only other teachers at higher or lower levels in the occupational hierarchy but also a variety of influential groups within and beyond education. Changing interdependencies and "the interweaving of...aims and activities" as well as the "immanent dynamics" (Mennell and Goudsblom, 1998, p. 120) of potentially conflict-ridden relationships are central to PE teachers' thoughts and deeds. Relationships of power may be more-or-less clear cut and have a more-or-less direct bearing upon the ideas and practices of teachers, depending upon their position amidst the plethora of hierarchies that exist within any occupational grouping.

It is also important to bear in mind that power balances "are dynamic and continually in flux" (Murphy *et al.*, 2000). Teachers' positions within departments, within schools, even within professional bodies, frequently change. Indeed, the position and influence of teachers as an occupational grouping can be seen to change over time in relation to the sports lobby, Government and even the medical profession, for example. The point is, then, that noting the relational character of power and the "various constellations in the balance of power" (Mennell and Goudsblom, 1998, p. 123) helps one understand how, in what circumstances, as well as in which directions, the influence of ideologies in the thinking of individuals and/or groups of PE teachers is likely to change.

In one sense, therefore, the study of PE teachers' "philosophies" is a study of power-ratios and power balances — that is, of the constraints surrounding PE teachers by virtue of their professional roles. The concepts of power-ratios and power balances help make sense of the tendency, highlighted by Elias, for specific groups to utilise knowledge for practical purposes (Mennell and Goudsblom, 1998). The fortune of particular ideologies may well vary or fluctuate with the professional and political fortune of the group adhering to them (Mannheim, 1960). In this vein, it may be useful to see PE teachers in a similar light to that which Elias (1993) throws upon Mozart; that is to say, as more-or-less dependent outsiders in political and professional contexts. Thus, PE teachers are tied to the views of the day, whether or not they want wholeheartedly to endorse them, and, at least in order to "get on", so to speak, PE teachers are more or less "obliged" to adopt the ideology/ies of the day.

Thus, the argument goes, the figurations that PE teachers are enmeshed in can be expected to have ramifications for the way in which PE teachers conceptualise their subject. Consequently, this book seeks to demonstrate how PE teachers' "philosophies" might be understood as part of the structure and dynamics of the chains of interdependency in which they find themselves. For, as intimated earlier, it is likely that "philosophies" at the level of practice have far more to do with habituses and the contexts of practice than, for example, root meanings of PE *as a concept*, as traced by educational philosophers, and as much to do with pragmatism as the influence of ideologies of PE inherited over the last half-century or so.

In this chapter, I have suggested that a figurational sociological approach to making sense of PE teachers' "philosophies" holds out more promise than a (traditional) philosophical perspective. Characteristic of analytical philosophy, McNamee (1998, p. 81) observes, is the tendency to proceed in argumentation "as if the logic of [the] analysis carries itself forward to a conclusion in the minds of any *reasonable* person" (emphasis added). These "reasonable" people include, of course, PE teachers — regardless of their practical context, for example their newness, the management style of their heads of department, the traditions of the department and the school, and so on. It is apparent that a philosophical approach to understanding the origins and bases of knowledge contains within it a tendency to reduce the search for definitions of the nature and purposes of PE to ideal-types. Those who adopt this approach thus engage in debate at the level of abstract ideas alone, as if ideas interact with each other. Philosophers of PE are, then, prone to "the pervasive tendency to reduce processes conceptually to states" (Mennell and Goudsblom, 1998, p. 37). From such a perspective, social phenomena, such as PE, are inevitably treated as being static: as something that has evolved into its final form with the task being to establish the defining features of that final form. A philosophical perspective, it is argued, involves an in-built tendency towards conceptualising PE in terms of an identifiable essence rather than a shifting set of practices more-or-less favoured by PE teachers who, in turn, hold more-or-less ideological conceptions of PE inevitably circumscribed by context. In portraying themselves as completely detached pursuers of abstract knowledge, philosophers of education might intentionally or otherwise be guilty of camouflaging what, in fact, amount to normative accounts of education. The ideal-type philosophies of professional philosophers of PE may themselves be more adequately viewed as lying on a continuum of detachment, which, at the negative pole, would amount to nothing more or less than what might be termed justificatory ideologies.

Interestingly, Mannheim (1960, p. 251) might be describing the relationship between the academic philosophy of PE and the "philosophies" of PE teachers when he describes the commonplace tendency toward "talking past one another":

> although they are more-or-less aware that the person with whom they are discussing the matter represents another group, and that it is likely that his (*sic*) mental structure as a whole is quite different when a concrete thing is being discussed, they speak as if their differences were confined to the specific question at issue around which their present disagreement crystallized. They overlook the fact that their antagonist differs from them in his whole outlook, and not merely in his opinion about the point under discussion.

However, in the case of the philosophy of PE, it is not simply a matter of academics and teachers "talking past one another", not least because in one sense PE teachers are not *talking* much (in the sense of philosophising) about PE at all. This point is central: most teachers simply *do* PE. To the extent that they can be identified, PE teachers' "philosophies" are identified implicitly in the practice of PE teaching. The extent to which PE teachers' "philosophies" bear any resemblance to academic philosophies of PE is an empirical question.

There is a second reason why it would be an oversimplification to talk about PE academics and teachers as "talking past one another", for educational philosophers *are* dealing with substantive issues. The point is that they are debating the substantive issue of what PE is at an abstract level — PE as a concept — rather than engaging with the reality of PE as practice. It is not so much that they talk past but that they simply are not talking on the same wavelength as PE teachers. Thus, it only becomes possible to make sense of PE teachers' "philosophies" if analysis is not restricted simply to ideas themselves or to the dictates of PE policy makers as reflected, for example, in the National Curriculum for Physical Education.

The figurational conception of people and their thinking is a conception of people diametrically opposed to that which has come to dominate intellectual history and epistemology since the Renaissance (Mennell and Goudsblom, 1998). The latter might be characterised, as Elias puts it, as a conception of a human being as a "We-less I". This is a conception of people in relation to knowledge as "a single thinking mind inside a sealed container from which one looks out and struggles to fish for knowledge of the objects in the 'external worlds'" (Mennell and Goudsblom, 1998, p. 33). It is important to acknowledge in passing, however (and especially in a sociological study of people's "philosophies"), that "this sense of the self inside its container looking out is very real as a mode of self-experience in modern societies" (p. 33). In a nutshell, this is why PE teachers' "philosophies" cannot be reduced to philosophy per se — nor, for that matter, to psychology. The knowledge and ideas of PE teachers cannot be explained by studying either the ideas themselves or the teacher (him- or herself) in isolation. Knowledge, for figurationalists, needs to be conceptualised as an *aspect* of interdependencies. Thus, PE teachers' thoughts, as well as their teaching behaviours, can only be fully understood when located in the figurations they form with each other – as inescapably *interdependent* people.

The outline of figurational sociology and the sociology of knowledge offered in this chapter is intended to explain why the approach adopted in this study will be in the vein of what Mennell and Goudsblom (1998, p. 28) describe as "Elias's characteristic trick": that is, "to turn what have traditionally been regarded as philosophical problems into sociological questions susceptible to theoretical-empirical investigation".

To bring this chapter to a close – and in the light of the above outline of a sociological approach to the ostensibly philosophical issue of knowledge – I want to offer a brief outline of how I intend to employ the two terms central to this sociological exploration of PE teachers' views: namely *philosophy* and *ideology*.

Philosophy
The term "philosophy" has a lexicographic sense, which broadly centres upon the rational principles underlying a putative knowledge base; and it will be the academic sense of philosophy that is utilised when describing educational philosophy in the section on academic ideology. It is important to note, however, that use of the term "philosophy" when talking of the viewpoint of teachers shares more in common with the taken-for-granted, everyday usage of the term: that is to say, one's view of "how things should be" – as might be illustrated at a conversational level by a phrase such as "my philosophy of PE is..." When describing the views of PE teachers, this represents, as the philosopher Antony Flew (1984, p. vii) indicates, use of the term "philosophy" "in a perfectly reputable and *useful* sense" (emphasis added):

> In this sense philosophy is a matter of standing back a little from the ephemeral urgencies to take an aphoristic overview that usually embraces both value-commitments and beliefs about the general nature of things.

Placing the term "philosophy" in quotation marks will be taken to represent this kind of aphoristic or everyday overview of the nature and purposes of PE by teachers whilst, at the same time, distinguishing such "philosophies" from the kinds of (ostensibly) abstract and rational arguments associated with academic philosophising. Indeed, as indicated earlier (Chapter 1 n. 1), and as this book endeavours to demonstrate, it would be more appropriate, sociologically speaking, to utilise the term "habitus" in preference to that of "philosophy", precisely because PE teachers' thoughts on the nature and purposes of PE tend not to be *constructed* in any substantial sense. Rather, they frequently appear as subconscious, slowly developing, predispositions that are revealed as *intuitions* more than conscious constructions per se. Nonetheless, and notwithstanding this caveat, the term "philosophy" will suffice here for the reasons already alluded to. In the case of PE teachers, their "philosophies" of PE may well—indeed are more likely to—be constructed as much in the midst of "ephemeral urgencies" as when stood back or "detached" from the hurly-burly of the day-to-day realities of teaching. Thus, whilst it will incorporate a summary of genuine philosophical attempts to make sense of the nature and purposes of PE, the book will, for the most part, utilise the term "philosophy" in its more "everyday" sense to describe the concise and pithy but, nevertheless, frequently intuitive overviews of the nature and purposes of PE held by teachers.

Although a precise picture of the conception, or "philosophy", of PE that each teacher wants to defend might not be readily identifiable, nor clear-cut, nor specific, the (ideological) contours are likely to be more-or-less visible. Particularly salient may be the most visible dimension of teachers' views on PE, namely what they *take for granted*: what appears to them as self-evident. In this regard, their early sporting and PE experiences, their undergraduate and postgraduate training, but also the circumstances in which they find themselves teaching (both at the macro and micro levels of their networks), as well as the constraints imposed upon them by the National Curriculum, might all combine to encourage a particular orientation, or view, towards PE and may well be reflected in the common-sense or taken-for-granted aspects of their "philosophies".

Ideology
Through the twentieth century, sociological uses of the term "ideology" have developed away from what have been termed (Mann, 1983) evaluatively *neutral* conceptions—characteristic of lexicographic definitions such as "a body or system of ideas"

(*Chambers*..., 1990) — towards definitions that incorporate pejorative and thus evaluatively *negative* connotations, "implying false or mistaken notions" (Mann, 1983, p. 164). Hence, standard sociological usages of the term have tended to qualify the concept of ideology (as "a general system of ideas") to incorporate notions of "falsehood and distortion generated by more or less unconscious motivations" (Flew, 1984, p. 162). Specifically figurational uses of the term ideology can be taken to embrace the habits and dispositions characteristic of habitus.

It is a central tenet of this book that much of the "knowledge" incorporated into, and thus constituent of, PE teachers' "philosophies" is, in fact, ideological; that is to say, it is by degrees more-or-less mythical (Dunning, 1999), more-or-less false, more-or-less distorted. Whilst by the late twentieth century ideologies per se may be said to "have absorbed a good deal of *factual*...knowledge" (Elias; cited in Mennell and Goudsblom, 1998, p. 32; emphasis added) they are, nonetheless, best viewed as located along a continuum between involvement and detachment (Mennell and Goudsblom, 1998). From this perspective, Dunning (1992, p. 178) observes that, whilst ideologies "differ in their degrees of reality-congruence...they always...contain a mythical component", making them what Elias would have termed "an amalgam of realistic observations and collective fantasies" (Elias; cited in Mennell and Goudsblom, 1998, p. 227). From such a perspective, it is argued in this book that, when PE teachers reveal their thoughts on the purposes of PE, they "bear the stamp of higher...[or] lesser detachment or involvement" (Elias; cited in Mennell and Goudsblom, 1998, p. 218) and in the process reveal degrees of "reality-congruence".

The distortions characteristic of ideological thinking range, for Mannheim (1960, p. 49), "all the way from conscious lies to half-conscious and unwitting disguises; from calculated attempts to dupe others to self-deception". What marks out differing views about the nature and purposes of PE as ideology — rather than as deception — is that they are not seen as "calculated lies" but, for the most part, as a consequence of the social situation teachers find themselves in (Mannheim, 1960): that is to say, on a continuum "between a simple lie at one pole, and an error, which is the result of a distorted and faulty conceptual apparatus, at the other" (Mannheim, 1960, p. 54).

It is important to note that ideologies, as Dunning (1992, p. 187) says of theories in general, "become fashionable for a greater or lesser period of time for extra-scientific reasons" and frequently this leads to an "uncritical submission to the authority and prestige of the dominant standards" (Elias; cited in Mennell and Goudsblom, 1998, p. 231). Mannheim (1960) draws our attention to the empirical tendency for ideologies to develop in conflict situations as a defence of, or attack upon, something or other — hence their propensity to distort. In this vein, Elias (cited in Mennell and Goudsblom, 1998, p. 227) points out that people:

> work and live in a world in which almost everywhere groups, small and great, including their own groups, are engaged in a struggle for position and often enough for survival, some trying to rise and better themselves in the teeth of strong opposition, some who have risen before trying to hold on to what they have, and some going down.

Given the social "fact" that diverse and multifaceted societies contain a plurality of ideologies, education and PE might be expected to contain a range of ideologies and vested interests expressed through a variety of discourses (Penney and Evans, 1997). In the case of this study of teachers' views, the significance of discourse as a manifestation of ideology is made apparent in Elias's observation that the "ways in which individuals of a group experience whatever affects their senses, the meaning which it has for them, depends on the standard forms for dealing with, and of thinking and speaking about, these phenomena" (Elias; cited in Mennell and Goudsblom, 1998, p. 218). This is a point worth dwelling upon, for whether student, teacher-trainee or head of department, all will be well aware of the continued prevalence of the notion of "traditional" PE.

Before proceeding any further, the crucial distinction between the concepts of ideology and discourse merits elaboration. According to Kirk (1992a, p. 23), discourse "refers to the ways in which people communicate their understanding of their own and others' activities, and of events in the world around them". This, for Johns, Gilbert and Shuttleworth (1994, p. 11), constitutes "the tacitly and explicitly governed pattern of language [employed] to portray what we view as our social reality". In a nutshell, then, discourses in PE are the multiplicity of ways in which those involved with the subject communicate something of what—for their part—PE *means* or *is about*: its nature and its purposes. Discourses are aspects of the processes by which ideologies are not only articulated but also developed. Discourse not only reveals the user's fundamental beliefs and values—about the nature and purposes of PE—it also serves to filter and form his or her thought processes at the same time; it does not simply reflect thinking, it is part of thinking itself. Although, as indicated earlier, several writers view discourse as reflecting ideology and as the embodiment of ideological work (Johns *et al.*, 1994; Kirk, 1992a), from a figurational sociological perspective it is more precise to view discourse as the work of "doing" ideology. On this view, discourse is best conceptualised as an *aspect* of the ideologies found among particular groups, rather than in the reified terms suggested by the claim that discourse embodies ideology. Conceptualising discourse in this way, it is argued, overcomes any tendency to view discourse and ideology as separate entities.

Conclusion

It can readily be seen, then, that in order to make sense of PE teachers' "philosophies" it becomes necessary to identify and make overt the ideological underpinnings of PE teachers' discourses, especially those practices that "involve the exercise of power to maintain the status quo" (Prain and Hickey, 1995, p. 78). To make sense of teachers' "philosophies", ideologies and the discourses that manifest them, the former need to be viewed in context: that is to say, in the particular figurations that make particular interpretations of PE more likely than others. This is what is characteristically meant when one refers to adopting the sociology of knowledge. The task of making sense of PE teachers' "philosophies" is, however, reserved for Chapter 6. In the meantime, Chapter 5 will outline these "philosophies" and the ideological themes identifiable therein.

3

Ideological Themes in Physical Education

In this portion of the book I want to provide an outline of the ideological themes that have been more-or-less prominent in the history of PE as a subject in the state-school system and, more particularly, secondary PE. It is worth reminding ourselves that, whilst they will be referred to as ideological themes, some (and especially the "academic" theme) have their roots in the philosophy of education and, as such, are nominally more philosophical than ideological. This notwithstanding, it is also worth remembering that (as suggested in Chapter 2), sociologically speaking, all the themes are more adequately described as ideological themes. This is because, far from being straightforwardly abstract, theoretical and impartial in nature, all themes — even the academic theme — are more-or-less idealised and mythical conceptions of PE, however systematic they appear and regardless of where their theoretical roots lie (for example, academia or public school traditions). Indeed, I am going on to suggest that at the "grass-roots" level of teaching PE these apparently reasoned systems of ideas are, in truth, aphoristic overviews that bear the clear imprint of strong value commitments and beliefs on the part of teachers. This, as I have already indicated, is why when referring to teachers' "philosophies" the term is placed in quotation marks to indicate the manner in which the supposedly rational thoughts of the teachers are, in sociological terms, better seen as ideological in nature — that is to say, by degrees, more-or-less mythical, more-or-less distorted.

Ideological Themes in Physical Education

Whilst there appear to be as many everyday "philosophies" of PE as there are PE teachers, two ideological themes dominate the history of PE: the pre-World War II (WWII) ideology of fitness and health and the post-war sporting (or "traditional games") ideology.

Contemporarily, "Many debates about the nature and future direction of physical education" continue, according to Penney (1998, p. 117), to revolve around these two allegedly "distinct and competing sets of interests" (see, for example, Penney, Clarke and Kinchin, 2002). Nonetheless, other ideologies besides those of sport and health have emerged with greater or lesser prominence over the last 30 years or so — including those that might be termed "sport for all" and "academic" ideologies. During this period both ideologies have become sufficiently prominent to begin to rival the more salient ideologies of sport and health. Since the late 1960s/early 1970s, in particular, an "academic" ideology has become increasingly discernible and influential (Carroll, 1994, 1998; Reid, 1996a, 1996b, 1997) to the extent that it shows signs of becoming a "new orthodoxy" within PE, particularly at secondary-school level (Green, 2001; Reid, 1996a;).

Latterly (from roughly the 1970s onwards), however, a substantially amended version of the health ideology has resurfaced (in the form of "health-related exercise" [HRE]) to vie with a renewed emphasis upon sport and team games as well as the academic and "sport for all" ideologies, for ideological ascendancy in PE. The growth of HRE and examinations in PE provided a particularly significant challenge to the pre-eminence of sport and "traditional games". Despite this, recent developments suggest that the health and academic ideologies have been unable to depose, let alone displace, the sporting ideology. Indeed, political intervention since the mid-1990s has encouraged a re-emphasis upon sport, and particularly "traditional games", as the core of PE, and there is no clear evidence that the most recent staging post in the turbulent history of the National Curriculum for Physical Education — signalled by the Curriculum 2000 review (Qualifications and Curriculum Authority [QCA], 1999) — has done anything to shift this emphasis. This is a matter I will return to in the concluding chapter.

Before examining the everyday "philosophies" of PE teachers (in Chapter 4), I want to deal with each of the ideologies in greater depth. For the sake of clarity these will, in broad terms, be presented chronologically as state schooling emerged and developed (in the nineteenth century) and PE as we know it today began to take shape in the early decades of the twentieth century.

The Ideology of Health

Despite the fact that many of the sons of the middle classes were revelling in the increasingly central position sport was coming to occupy in the public school education of young gentlemen towards the end of the nineteenth century, the lot of the children of the masses was wholly different. Although elementary schoolchildren could be instructed in drill (following the 1870 Education Act), this was permissible rather than mandatory. Indeed, "Working-class boys had little enough physical education in school, working-class girls usually had none at all" (Holt, 1989, p. 118). This rudimentary physical training, which formed the developmental origins of a nascent PE in the state system (in the form of drill for the most part), initiated what was to be a long association between PE and concern for health and fitness. Thus, in the shape of physical "training", PE became a significant element of the curriculum of state elementary schools in the early years of the twentieth century – a form of therapy intended to remedy the physical ailments and defects of young children (a significant public issue around the turn of the century) through disciplined exercise (Bray, 1991; Holt, 1989; Williams, 1988).

The publication of several syllabi, between 1909 and 1933, confirmed the role of PE as "an arm of the School Medical Service" (Kirk, 1992a, p. 129). In ideological, as well as practical, terms little of significance altered between the wars. The 1933 syllabus, despite including games, swimming and dancing as well as gymnastics (Bray, 1991), reiterated a medico-health rationale for PE as a form of training to remedy physical defects. As such, the syllabus was a "confirmation of the past" (Kirk, 1992a, p. 130) emphasising, as it did, physical education's "*de facto* status as health education" (p. 131) in schools.

To all intents and purposes, the fledgling PE functioned as an adjunct to the medical profession during the first half of the twentieth century. The emphasis upon remedial exercise assisted the work of school medical officers by seeking to inculcate healthy habits and healthy pursuits in young children. What amounted in the elementary schools to "gym for the masses" constituted "an after-the-event cure, or at least treatment, for particular manifestations of poor health" (Kirk, 1992a, p. 18). At the same time, PE was also expected to ensure a healthier and more disciplined male workforce and potential army, as well as stronger, healthier mothers for future generations. As a result, "military drill fleshed out with some general exercise" (Holt, 1989, p. 139), together with a little therapeutic gymnastics, was considered to be all that working-class boys and girls required.

The "rational recreation" movement (preachers, teachers, philan-thropists and other "dedicated improvers of the young" [Holt, 1989, p. 139]) had sought, since the 1880s, to involve working-class boys and youths in games (such as football), which they believed would have similarly beneficial moral and spiritual effects to those claimed for the sons of the middle classes. Despite this, the roots of the remedial, body-conditioning strand of school PE remained well and truly in place by the time of World War I. Consequently, a more restricted physical-fitness oriented, therapeutic notion of health (with a clear emphasis upon the remedial "health" function of physical activity) prevailed, dominating PE within the state school system until after World War II (WWII).

Notwithstanding the growing encouragement from various groups (including the Board of Education) for the inclusion of a broad range of activities, in addition to gymnastics, in physical "education", the underlying reality remained less encouraging. Although the emerging modern sporting forms had taken hold in public schools by the latter stages of the nineteenth century, the majority of youngsters were receiving instruction in repetitive gymnastic drill-type activities in elementary schools until WWII. General exercises, rather than games, were the staple diet of working-class children. To the extent that physical training was included in the education of lower-class youngsters, the aim was merely to minimise or remedy economic and military deficiencies caused by an unhealthy and unfit population (Alderson and Crutchley, 1990). Indeed, the kinds of exercise recommended were those "defined by medical practitioners in medical terms" (Kirk, 1992a, p. 129) — thereby reflecting the manner in which a process of medicalisation (that was already well under way in wider society) was taking hold in PE in the early part of the twentieth century (Waddington and Murphy, 1992).

The Ideology of Sport and "Traditional" Team Games

After WWII, and alongside the introduction of compulsory school-ing, the paramedical role—characteristic of the kind of physical *training* that PE had remained in practice—was gradually under-mined by the rapid growth and burgeoning influence of team games in PE. This was largely due to the large influx of games-oriented male teachers (keen to duplicate the alleged character benefits of games playing in the public schools) into the newly emerging secondary schools (Kirk, 1992a) and, particularly, the grammar schools (who frequently looked to the public school system for their academic and social models). This significant move towards concern with physical *education*, rather than merely physical *training*, encompassed a broader concern for moral and spiritual development (Kirk, 1992a) and the alleged character benefits of games playing. Consequently, the main challenge to "the early biologically oriented physical training model" became "the attractiveness of the play movement and a dedication to teach-ing social values through games and sports" (Park, 1994, p. 64).

Despite the existence of a public school "games" tradition, as well as the well-established popularity of competitive sports among adult participants and spectators alike, the competitive team games and sports (that "had been part of the cultural fabric of British life" [Kirk, 1992a, p. 84] for almost one hundred years by the end of WWII) "did not form a substantial part of PE programmes in the state sector until the introduction of mass secondary schooling in the late-1940s" (Kirk, 1992a, p. 84). Nonetheless, from the 1950s onwards, the popularity of games (and sport) within state schools increased rapidly, coming to occupy the ideological high ground of the subject as both "the core of physical education and the largest part of the programme" (Kirk, 1992a, p. 84). In the process, sport (and particularly team games) attained the epithet of "traditional" PE. As Houlihan (1991) points out, the dominant ideology within PE since the 1944 Education Act has been "traditional physical education and its central concern [and justification] the enhancement of sports performance" (Houlihan, 1991, p. 234).

In relation to the notion of "traditional" PE, it is worth noting that—when viewed over the century of PE's existence—the term would be more appropriately applied to exercise for health and fitness than games and sport for character development. Despite this, the somewhat mythical[1] epithet "traditional" has nevertheless formed a taken-for-granted aspect of much discourse surrounding PE ever since.

It is also worthy of note that, in marked contrast to what was happening in boys' PE, the early years of the twentieth century witnessed the development of a quite distinctive female tradition for privately educated middle-class girls. The combination of health-enhancing therapeutic gymnastics, with the character training and all-round physical vigour believed to characterise team games, were to be found increasingly in the new and more exclusive girls schools, staffed with games mistresses from the growing and celebrated colleges of Madame Bergman-Osterberg (Holt, 1989). Nonetheless, a number of girls' public boarding schools closely modelled themselves on the boys' public schools of the period, and it is noteworthy that "it was in the emphasis on games where the imitation of boys' public schools became most slavish" (Hargreaves, 1994, p. 65). The second-tier, relatively status-inferior, girls' public schools had replicated developments in boys' grammar schools of the mid-nineteenth century and imitated the boys' "superior" education in a manner not dissimilar to that of boys' PE in the new secondary schools.

As the "traditional" games-based curriculum developed within post-WWII boys' PE, the paramedical, restorative role of PE rescinded. Gradually, it was undermined by a combination of the influx of games-oriented men into the newly emerging secondary schools and the growth in popularity of educational gymnastics favoured and championed by the girls' PE tradition (Kirk, 1992a). As a consequence, the period after WWII, particularly from 1950 onwards, saw competitive team games and sports emerge at the mass level to form the core of both boys and girls secondary PE (Kirk, 1992a). Ever since then, "school PE programmes have been grounded in the development of sports skills and participation in competitive team games" (Macdonald and Kirk, 1996, p. 63). Thus, in the second half of the twentieth century secondary-school PE programmes have gradually become very similar — revolving

---

[1] For figurationalists, mythical thinking is typically a central feature of ideologies per se (see Chapter 2).

around team games and a skill-based pedagogy. So much so, that they can justifiably be said to represent what Placek *et al.* (1995) have identified (in the USA) as "an unplanned and unrecognised national physical education curriculum", tantamount to a kind of de facto national curriculum.

Whilst an explicit and, as Kirk (1992a) terms it, "direct" concern for fitness for health was relegated to the margins of PE during the post-WWII period, in truth, the development represented a reorientation of fitness (towards sports performance) rather than an abandonment of concern for fitness as such. The armed forces physical training instructors (PTIs), and (from the 1950s) men returning from National Service, brought with them a concern for (functional) fitness interpreted as the capacity to perform work based on strength and stamina and, thus, in terms of its application to sports performance. The approach of these PTIs, who formed the backbone of PE after WWII, was grounded in a medical view of the function of exercise for health, in the form of an application of the new scientific knowledge derived primarily from the fields of exercise physiology and bio-mechanics (Bray, 1991; Kirk, 1992a). Where they persisted, the compensatory or remedial forms of exercise (recommended in Ministry of Education publications in the early 1950s) were concerned more with the all-round development of children through a broad range of activities (Bray, 1991) than with the "traditional para-medical, remedial role" of physical training of the elementary school period (Kirk, 1992a, p. 135). Thus, by the middle of the 1950s, the games ideology (increasingly incorporating a concern for the utilisation of scientific principles in the improvement of sporting performance) was in the process of dominating PE in the nascent secondary system. Hence, despite the emerging pre-eminence of games, there lay within this tradition a strong theme of concern for functional fitness — concern for fitness in terms of strength and stamina and its application to sports performance rather than health. As Kirk (1992a, p. 144) observed, "the defining aim of any programme that deserved the label physical education was the improvement of the physical and physiological performance of an individual".

The "traditional" model of PE — incorporating physical activities such as gymnastics but dominated by sport and team games — became the convention in the grammar and secondary schools of the 1960s and the comprehensive schools of the 1970s and beyond. Nevertheless, whilst the shape of PE appeared very much like a continuation of the "traditional" model, the subject, as it has developed in the last 30 or so years, cannot be understood purely in terms of the triumph of a sporting ideology over a health (and fitness) ideology. Not only is it necessary to note the re-emergence of a health ideology, it is also crucial to chart the impact of other ideologies and particularly those inherent in the liberal educational philosophy that came to dominate theorising about education from the 1960s onwards. What might be termed a growing academicisation of secondary education over the last 40 years or so can be seen to have had profound consequences for PE, not least in terms of the process of review and reconstruction required by physical educationalists in order to justify the inclusion of their subject in the increasingly academically oriented secondary-school curriculum.

Thus, alongside the two central ideologies of health and fitness and sport the emergence of several more-or-less marginal ideologies can be discerned over the last 30 or so years. The most prominent of these developments has been the appearance and consolidation (Reid, 1996a, 1996b, 1997) of an academic ideology.

The Academic Ideology

The growth in educational theory after WWII was interdependent with the introduction of compulsory secondary education and the concomitant development of teacher training. From the 1960s onwards, the pre-eminent form of theorising about the nature and purposes of education came to be that of liberal educational philosophy. This post-war philosophical tradition in Britain — associated, particularly, with the work of Richard Peters and Paul Hirst in the 1960s and 1970s — provided the template for much subsequent *academic* reflection upon, analysis of and justification for PE vis-à-vis the remainder of the formal school curriculum (Arnold, 1997; Carr, 1997; O'Hear, 1981; Reid 1996a, 1996b, 1997). The "Peters-Hirst" approach (Carr, 1997) to philosophising about education is based upon the premise that education has fundamentally to do with *knowledge* and that knowledge, in turn, is essentially theoretical or intellectual. On this view what distinguishes education "from other forms of socialisation, formation

41

and training" is its concern with the "initiation of pupils into a broad range...of forms of rational knowledge and enquiry" (Carr, 1997, p. 196), which, it is claimed, are inevitably intellectual. A corollary of this perspective is that the acquisition of (theoretical) knowledge can only be manifested, and its acquisition assessed, in written or spoken form (Reid, 1996a, 1996b). On this conceptualisation, education is interpreted as being "essentially *academic*" (Reid, 1996b, p. 95; emphasis in the original). The widespread preeminence of this perspective within academia—and teacher training especially—has, in effect, left physical educationalists with two options:

> firstly, to acknowledge its [PE] traditionally non-academic and therefore non-educational [or, at best, marginal] status; or, secondly, to argue that despite appearances, the physical activities which comprise the familiar physical education curriculum can somehow be shown to have academic significance and thus educational worth. (Reid, 1996b, p. 95)

Thus, the increasing dominance of the analytical (Peters-Hirst) conception of education from the 1960s (Carr, 1997; Parry, 1998; McNamee, 1998; Reid, 1996b, 1997;) presented those teachers and academics who favoured the "traditional" de facto PE curriculum— in the games-oriented form in which it had developed—with a profound dilemma. PE had either to "undergo a radical change of identity and redefine itself as an academic subject in the school curriculum, or else acknowledge its incorrigibly marginal status" (Reid, 1997, p. 6). The liberal educational tradition has remained a more-or-less pre-eminent influence in educational theory since that period and consequently PE teachers have—notwithstanding their own experiences of, and intuitive preferences for, school PE as a *practical* subject—been professionally socialised (via teacher training as well as official and semi-official publications) into the "standard", academic ideology ever since.

In relation to the theme of this book, it is worth noting that, for Peters, Hirst and others at the academic level, the debate has been an ostensibly philosophical one (see the introduction to this chapter) about the *nature* and *value* of knowledge and education. However, it is far more likely that from the perspective of the PE teacher, the focus of concern has not been the nature of knowledge as such but rather about the implications of the dominance of an academic ideology for the lived reality of their jobs as PE teachers, such as the status of PE (and, by association, PE teachers), the struggle for resources, and their job security. To many physical educationalists — at all levels but particularly among PE academics and teacher-trainers — it has appeared evident that, "if the possession of academic credentials is a condition of entry to the mainstream" curriculum, then physical educationalists were, and for that matter remain, obliged to direct their subject away from "the familiar idea of the teaching and learning of practical physical activities" (Reid, 1996b, p. 95) and towards "academic" aspects of PE. In other words, PE would have to be reoriented towards intellectual and moral development *through* sport (particularly the allegedly scientific dimensions of the study of sport) rather than the *practice* of sport. According to Reid, a consequence of the broad acceptance of the "orthodox" liberal educational view of PE has been repeated calls for a greater emphasis upon "theory" within the subject at the expense of unreflective practice or "playing". The "new orthodoxy", as Reid (1996b, p. 102) terms it, has sought to "redefine physical education in terms of the opportunities which it provides for theoretical study" and, in doing so, has implicitly accepted the superiority of the kinds of knowledge that are expressed predominantly in written or verbal forms rather than by practical demonstration. If PE is not concerned with the acquisition and mastery of theoretical knowledge, the argument goes, it is — by the very nature of education — non-academic and thus non-educational.

The growing influence of the "academic" conceptualisation of education created a context in which physical educationalists were (and, indeed, continue to be) confronted by the kind of questions posed by Carr: "What is the *educational* value or significance of physical activity?" and "What part, if any, has physical education to play in the general education of a person?" (Carr, 1979, p. 91; emphasis added). It appears evident that physical educationalists, caught in the glare of the prevailing "academic" view of education, have been constrained — in order to continue to claim a place for their subject on the curriculum — to recognise the distinction between "the practical performance of physical activities and the propositional or theoretical knowledge which is related to them" (Reid, 1996b, p. 95) and then to assert the academic character of the knowledge promoted within PE.

Whether or not it is justifiable to claim that the "academic" option — that is to say, demonstrating the academic or intellectual significance of PE (what Reid labels the "standard" view of PE and what we might call the "academic ideology") — has acquired the status of a "new orthodoxy", it seems undeniable that a process of academicisation is well underway in PE. Several developments in recent years appear to confirm this: firstly, the dramatic growth of examinable PE (Carroll, 1998; Green, 2001; Reid, 1996a); secondly, the proliferation of PE/sports science degrees (Carroll, 1998); and thirdly, the widespread acceptance and adoption of the academicisation of PE in current curriculum and assessment policy (Reid, 1996a). Indeed, attempts to establish the academic credibility of PE are readily discernible in a range of official and semi-official definitions over the last 20 or so years, as well as in debates within various groups among the subject-community. Nowhere is the process of academicisation more clearly illustrated than by the conceptualisation of PE built into the template for NCPE, *Physical Education for Ages 5 to 16* (DES/WO, 1991, p. 5), as the *education* of young people "*in* and *through* the use and knowledge of the body and its movement" (emphases added). In this definition, the requisite theoretical or intellectual component has two discernible dimensions: firstly, knowledge, in the form of underlying principles, *about* the performance of physical activities ("*in* the use and knowledge of the body"); and, secondly, knowledge about other areas of allegedly valuable knowledge, such as morality, social and health education ("*through* the use and knowledge of the body") that PE is held to be well (according to some, uniquely) placed to deliver. Thus, over the last quarter of a century or so (Carr, 1997), the standard view of PE has been mobilised to justify both the use of physical activities to teach principles of moral or social education and also to teach the theoretical principles (such as the acquisition of skill or the contribution of exercise to health) upon which *practical* ability and performance, as well as involvement, in sport is said to be founded.

In practice, physical educationalists have sought, in particular, to utilise one of the traditional moral or personal and social education justifications for physical activity — that of character development — as the main plank of "educational" justification for the subject. According to Evans and Davies (1986, p. 18), the PE profession "has both historically and contemporaneously paraded its social objectives and socializing functions publicly among its professional aims". What marks the academic, or "standard", view of the contribution of PE to personal and social education (PSE) out, and sets it apart from the pre-Peters–Hirst position, is the emphasis upon initiation into the alleged intellectual components of moral behaviour and character development via physical activities. This stands in opposition to the osmotic view of moral education — as simply permeating the character of young boys — that was associated with the public-school games tradition dominant in secondary PE immediately after WWII. The continuing influence of these two strands of thought can be readily identified in the titles of various publications relating to the supposed spiritual, moral, social and cultural dimensions of physical education (see, for example, Blake, 1996; Laker, 1996a, 1996b).

With the above points in mind, what I have termed the "academic" ideology — that is to say, the belief among teachers that PE aids pupils' intellectual as well as their personal, social and moral development — can, for explanatory purposes, be further subdivided into two aspects: that which I will label PSE because it fits neatly with the school subject of that name;[2] and intellectual development, which, according to at least one commentator (Reid, 1996a, 1996b, 1997), is rapidly acquiring the mantle of a "new orthodoxy" among physical educationalists.

One aspect of the alleged role of PE in intellectual development is worthy of particular attention: that of examinable PE. One of the more dramatic developments in secondary PE over the last 30 years has been the rapid growth of examinations; particularly at General Certificate of Secondary Education (GCSE) and Advanced ("A") level (Carroll, 1998; Green, 2001; Reid, 1996a). GCSE PE, for example, more than doubled in terms of the number of examinees in the five-year period up to 1997 (Office for Standards in Education [OFSTED], 1998) and continues to be an increasingly strong feature of secondary PE (Green, 2001). The rapid growth of examinations

---

[2] "Personal and Social Education" has, in government documents and professional publications in recent years, been extended to incorporate "health" issues and, consequently, has been retitled "Personal, Social and Health Education" (PSHE) (see the Qualifications and Curriculum Authority [QCA] 1999).

in PE (Carroll, 1998; Green, 2001) lends weight, on the face of it, to the claim that the academic (or "standard") view of education, which has flourished in education at all levels since the 1960s, is in the ascendancy, not least insofar as contemporary justifications for PE among academics, teacher-trainers and even teachers commonly make use of academic justifications to bolster their subject's standing.

Perhaps the most interesting aspect of the "academic" ideology, for a sociology of knowledge, has been the way in which it has become intertwined with other ideologies and has, in turn, impacted upon them. This development is neatly illustrated in the re-emergence within PE discourse of the health ideology.

The Re-emergence of the Health Ideology

The pre-eminence of the "games tradition" in secondary schooling after WWII meant that, by the 1960s, games had become established as the dominant influence within PE (Kirk, 1992a; Tinning, 1991). Nonetheless, the "rhetoric of 'health'" (Park, 1994, p. 64) — advocating the health-promoting benefits of exercise — continued to be a regular and significant inclusion in the objectives of PE (Bray, 1991; Tinning, 1991). What Kirk (1992a, p. 138) terms this "lingering but residual influence in physical education discourse" was enhanced by broader developments within the PE subject-community, in the international sporting arena and throughout Western societies at large, during the second half of the twentieth century.

Around the same period that "games" were becoming firmly established upon the ideological high ground of secondary PE, developments beyond education — a dramatic growth in the allegedly preventable and "self-inflicted" illnesses that were said to reflect contemporary lifestyles and were perceived as having replaced the conquered "infectious" diseases as the *bête noire* of the medical professions (Colquhoun, 1991) — were facilitating the re-emergence and re-establishment of the "health" ideology in the PE subject-community. Growing concern in the 1960s and 1970s with the dramatic rise in so-called "lifestyle diseases" (for example, cancer and heart disease) coupled with an increased awareness of, and concern regarding, the issue of health-related fitness, had the effect of focusing the attention of "scientists" among the emergent

PE profession on the potential preventative role of PE in relation to hypokinetic (under-exercising) diseases. By the 1970s, the idea was well established — emanating primarily from medical discourse — that people living in modern, highly urbanised and industrial societies were in greater need of regular exercise than previous generations (American Alliance for Health, Physical Education, Recreation and Dance [AAHPERD], 1980; Kirk, 1992a) and that physical activity together with modifications in lifestyles could act as an effective preventative tool (Colquhoun, 1991, 1992; Colquhoun and Kirk, 1987).

By the 1980s, concern — especially among "professional" bodies with a vested interest (for example, AAHPERD in the USA and the Physical Education Association [PEA] in the UK) — began to focus upon levels of exercise that were sufficient to increase levels of fitness and improve health. The upshot of this process of amplification of the alleged "health crisis" by the medical profession was the development of an orthodoxy that came to dominate much PE discourse, at least in the form of academic and professional utterances. Subsequently, a relatively straightforward and taken-for-granted, medically oriented, analysis came to prevail in health and exercise discourse. In short, the "health crisis" provided a medico-health context for PE intervention (Kirk, 1992a; Tinning, 1991). According to Fox (1993), the extensive research literature available by the early 1990s contained a clear message for PE: namely, the necessity of establishing "the goal of promoting exercise for public health" as a main priority (Fox, 1993, p. 36). Indeed, not only was regular exercise presented as being self-evidently important in the fight against the so-called risk factors associated with coronary heart disease (Kirk, 1992a), it was also made clear that this commitment to exercise had to be of a type likely to be continued into adult life (Green, 1994). If exercise was to impact upon the health of the nation it had to be married to a lifelong commitment to participation (Almond, 1983; Armstrong, 1987; Armstrong and Welsman, 1997; Fox 1983a, 1983b).

The move towards health-related fitness (HRF) (or, as it has come to be referred to in academic circles, health-related exercise [HRE]) gathered momentum within PE throughout the 1970s. It represented not only a growth in influence of a health ideology but also a movement away from organised games. In truth, it was a movement more noticeable among academics than teachers. This notwithstanding, the "traditional games"-based curriculum came under increased pressure from several directions. The 1960s witnessed growing criticism of the alleged failure of PE to bring about the kinds of moral and character development in young people upon which it was premised. In addition, "traditional" PE, based around competitive team games, was alleged to have also failed to check, let alone reverse, the "drop-out" from leisure sport during mid-to-late adolescence (with the concomitant consequences for the physical and moral well-being of an allegedly increasingly delinquent youth population) highlighted by the Wolfenden Report (Central Council for Physical Recreation [CCPR], 1960). Included in this attack on the "functions" of PE was a continuation of earlier criticism regarding the demise of Britain's sporting success, linked analogously with Britain's diminishing worldwide political influence (Kirk, 1992a). Consequently, since the 1980s, one of the major developments in PE has been the rise of the health-based PE movement (Tinning, 1991), the most significant manifestation of which was HRE. An influential lobby has developed within the PE subject-community (and particularly at the level of academia) promulgating the supposed health benefits of regular exercise (see, for example, Almond, 1983, 1989; Armstrong, 1990; Armstrong and Welsman, 1997; Arnold, 1991; Biddle, 1987; Cale, 2000; Fairclough, Stratton and Baldwin, 2002; Fox, 1983a, 1983b; Harris and Cale, 1997). Thus, claims for a role for PE in the process of *educating* children about healthy and active lifestyles lay at the end of a chain of connections emanating from the apparent growth of hypokinetic or "lifestyle diseases" of the late twentieth century (Armstrong, 1990; Corbin, Metal-Corbin and Biddle, 1989; McGeorge, 1992).

During the last decade or so, HRE (under various names but most typically HRF) has become an integral part of PE curricula (Cale, 2000; Fairclough *et al.*, 2002; Underwood, Bird and Farmiloe, 1993) and has assumed increasing prominence in PE discourse (Colquhoun, 1992; Kirk, 1992a). Indeed, HRE is to be found in an ever-increasing majority of secondary-school PE curricula (Harris, 1994a). Consequently, by the end of the century, the PE subject-community had become characterised by an ever-increasing interest in the exercise levels, and attendant lifestyles, of school-age children (Armstrong, 1990; Armstrong and Welsman, 1997; Colquhoun,

1992; Fox, 1993; Green and Thurston, 2002).

It is noteworthy, then, that despite the growing significance of HRE in PE theory and HRF in PE practice, games continues to occupy a substantial place in PE — both in ideological terms and as a relative proportion of the total amount of PE time. Notwithstanding this observation, a growing acceptance of HRE (albeit with an emphasis upon *fitness*) on the part of teachers, as well as academics, was evident — confirming the ascendancy of the "health" ideology at the level of PE practice as well as theory. The last two decades of the twentieth century are held to have witnessed a significant shift in the theorising about and teaching of PE (Park, 1994): a sea change in the direction of an ideology of health on the part of academics, teacher-trainers and even, to a large extent, PE teachers themselves.

Whilst not readily discernible, nor perhaps as salient, as the ideological themes of health, sport and education, two other ideologies — those of "sport for all" (grouped here with what has been termed "education for leisure") and what I will refer to (after Siedentop, 1994) as "sport education" — are worthy of mention. Whilst these might be seen as relatively marginal ideologies, it is claimed that "education for leisure" and "sport for all" have been an often unrecognised but nonetheless significant dimension of PE teachers' "philosophies" and practices over the last two to three decades (see, for example, Roberts, 1995, 1996a, 1996b, 1997; Scraton, 1992). By the same token, in the case of sport education, it is claimed that this conception of PE may come to form a significant part of ideologies of the next decade or so (Almond, 1996; Penney *et al.*, 2002; Siedentop, 1994).

"Education for Leisure", "Sport for All" and the "New PE"

At the same time that the process of medicalisation (associated with the development of HRE) was taking hold in the discourse of PE, growing concern at governmental level with the ramifications of economic and social changes (Hendry, 1986; Scraton, 1995) was increasingly apparent. "Shifts in the work–leisure balance in society" alongside a "spectacular increase in unemployment, particularly among young people" (Hendry, 1986, p. 52) were, it is claimed, having a significant impact on the perceptions of many PE teachers regarding their aims (Hendry, 1986; Roberts, 1996b, 1997; Scraton, 1995). Roberts (1996b) describes how, since the 1960s, there have been major changes in young people's leisure styles, which have reflected their changed economic and social circumstances. By the mid-1980s, "preparation for leisure" was stated as a primary aim of PE teaching by every secondary school in Scraton's (1995) research. Indeed, according to Scraton, most teachers "recognised this as a changed emphasis throughout the 1970s and early-1980s", a fact that she also viewed as attributable to the increased leisure time associated with economic changes of the period.

The emphasis in much of this teaching of PE, according to Scraton (1995) and Roberts (1996b), was on enjoyment of a breadth of sports and physical activities in "preparation for participation in post-school leisure time" (Scraton, 1995, p. 113). Thus, over the course of the last three decades, PE teachers have increasingly made use of curricular and — to a lesser extent — extra-curricular PE to introduce young people to a wide variety of sports and physical activities (Mason, 1995; Office for National Statistics [ONS], 1999; Roberts, 1996a, 1996b; Scraton, 1995). Scraton (1995) and Roberts (1996b) observed a shift of emphasis among PE teachers in the 1970s and 1980s towards so-called "education for leisure". Such developments in PE teachers' practices, it is suggested, were underscored by a prevailing view that sport and physical activity offered a suitable means of combating allegedly emerging social "problems" such as youth vandalism and urban crime.

Collectively, the developing interest in HRE and a further, related development of the 1980s (the so-called "Teaching Games for Understanding" [TGFU] approach [Waring and Almond, 1995]), in conjunction with the general concern for the encouragement of "education for leisure" or "sport for all", became known during this period as the "new PE". For its part, TGFU was ostensibly a reaction against the domination not only of games in "traditional" PE curricula but also the allegedly didactic, skill-development approaches and emphases of "traditional" games-based PE. More particularly, it was presented by particular academics involved in teacher training as a response rooted in the perceived failure of traditional games teaching to secure wider participation among youngsters in games after school age and the relative failure to bring about marked improvement in their sporting abilities and thus likely continued participation (or "education for leisure"). The process of broadening the traditional curricula to meet the perceived "leisure" needs of young people ran alongside, and worked in the same direction as, concern with HRE. This growing interest among academics and teacher-trainers within the PE subject-community with the role of PE in promoting "health" articulated neatly with notions of "education for leisure" and "sport for all".

Thus, the "new PE" of the 1980s appears to have been of a piece with the broadening of the PE curriculum that increasingly manifested itself in "options" (or "activity choice" as OFSTED [1998] referred to it) within upper-school PE (15-16 year olds) in the 1970s and the "sport for all" policies of the government quango, the Sports Council, around the same time. Roberts (1995, 1996a) also highlighted what he took to be the changing "philosophies" and practices of PE teachers around this time. He observed that, whereas in the 1950s and 1960s "the physical education teachers who were in post had been literally trained to 'drill' pupils and offer a limited range of games" (Roberts, 1996b, p. 16), in the last 25 years teachers have been more likely to respond to youth trends (Roberts, 1995, 1996a, 1996b) and to adapt school sport "to young people's changing leisure styles" (Roberts, 1996b, p. 20). By extending the traditional games-oriented curriculum to incorporate individual and small group activities, offering so-called "option PE" for older pupils and by utilising the new sports centres being developed in the 1970s and 1980s (that would provide the venues and opportunities for children's later participation), PE teachers have, according to Roberts (1995, 1996a), placed "sport for all" ahead of competitive team sport. When measured in terms of encouraging recruitment into sport among young people, what Roberts (1995, 1996a, 1996b) terms the "success" of school sport over the last two decades was grounded in PE teachers' sensitivities to "youth's new social condition" and the concomitant changes in their leisure patterns (Green, 2002; Roberts, 1996b).

Notwithstanding the accuracy of Roberts's claims regarding the reorientation of PE towards what I am calling "education for leisure", it is worth adding a caveat. As Evans (1992, pp. 241-242) observed, changes in underlying ideologies, as reflected in the emergence and development of the so-called "new PE" philosophies in the 1980s, "reflected a radical shift in rather than a rejection of certain priorities in these teachers' philosophy of PE". Nonetheless, and despite this note of caution, it was indeed the case, according to Evans (1992), that the priorities of those teachers engaging in change:

> lay not so much with the identification and sponsorship of sport skills amongst the physically able children but rather with cultivating the physical well being, the talent, enjoyment and interest in sport of all the children in their care. (Evans, 1992, p. 242)

He added:

> The curriculum initiatives which these teachers had effected had involved substantial (radical) changes in their way of working and in what might be termed their operational ideology and some significant shifts in the priorities within their fundamental ideologies. (p. 242)

It is worth adding two further caveats at this point. Firstly, one might reasonably question the extent to which Evans is justified in claiming a *radical* shift in teachers' priorities, let alone whether this shift was commonplace across the broad range of PE teachers. At the same time, however, it is necessary to acknowledge that several prominent authors underscore the claim that many PE teachers did become concerned with what might broadly be termed, "education for leisure" and "sport for all" from the 1970s onwards. Secondly, with the previous point in mind and notwithstanding the relative success of the "new PE" and, in particular, its defining development over the last decade (Kirk, 1992a) — HRE — it would be a mistake to suggest that it had fatally undermined (or even radically shifted) the place of games and sport in "traditional" PE. In this regard, Roberts (1995, 1996a, 1996b) notes that games have maintained their prominent place on virtually all secondary PE curricula. Mason's (1995) Sports Council study into *Young people and sport* and Sport England's (2001) *Young people and sport in England 1999* support Roberts's (1996a) claim that team games and competitive sports generally remain "alive and well" in England's schools. Notwithstanding the growth of popularity of HRE in secondary PE, traditional team games and sports remained at the heart of the curriculum in the mid-1990s: "Neither PE teachers nor their colleagues had turned against Britain's traditional team sports"

(Roberts, 1995, p. 339). Despite claims to the contrary by successive Governments (see Department of National Heritage [DNH], 1995; Green, 2002; Roberts, 1996a, 1996b; Sport England, 2001), young people are continuing to experience a substantial amount of sport and team games in secondary PE — both in absolute terms and as a proportion of total curricular (as well as extra-curricular) time devoted to PE (Mason, 1995; Roberts, 1996a, 1996b; Sport England, 2001; Sports Council for Wales [SCW], 1995;). Thus, Roberts suggests, contrary to claims that there has been an unchecked decline in school sport it has, in fact, been a "success story" when viewed over the period of time since WWII and measured in terms of levels of participation. School sport has adapted (by broadening the PE curricula) to the broader trends in youth cultures since the 1970s, Roberts argues, because teachers "have been responsive and innovative, have known 'what works' with their pupils, and have ranked 'sport for all' ahead of producing winning teams" (1996b, p. 113). Roberts's final point is worthy of particular note in relation to claims regarding shifting or changing priorities among PE teachers: "The situation was not", Roberts (1995, p. 339) adds, that team games had been "dropped", but "rather that they had been joined by other activities in broader sports curricula than the traditional team games regime".

Whilst there is a clear sense in which the ideologies of "education for leisure" / "sport for all" and health could be said to share similar goals — for example, in terms of the purported desire to encourage in young people lifelong participation in physical activity — there was always a strand of thought in the former that might set it against the latter. "Education for leisure" can be seen, at least in part, as a forerunner of the contemporary ideology of "sport education" — initiation into sports, to be enjoyed for their own sake as a valued cultural practice, rather than as a means of promoting health.

"Sport Education" and the "Valued Cultural Practice"[3] of Sport

An increasingly prominent marginal ideology — at least in the academic and professional press — since the 1980s has been what

[3] Although they are more commonly referred to as "valued human practices" in the academic literature, I will continue to use the term "valued *cultural* practices" because of its more sociological associations and implications.

has become known as "sport education" (Penney *et al.*, 2002; Siedentop, 1994). The term emerged to reflect the notion that the "educational" function of PE should be seen as that of developing young people's knowledge and understanding of a valued aspect of their national culture, namely sport. The notion of sport education has emerged alongside a shift in recent years among a number of established educational philosophers (see, for example, Hirst, 1994) away from the academic ideology – whereby education was viewed principally as the initiation of young people into "forms of knowledge" as such – and towards education as initiation into "valued cultural practices". Whilst the valued cultural practices and academic conceptions of PE share a belief in the centrality of knowledge, as far as the former is concerned this is only knowledge in or *about* sport and not the inculcation of knowledge about other aspects of human practice (such as morality) *through* sport.

Thus, in many ways, the notion of valued cultural practices has come to provide the philosophical rationale for those favouring a view of PE as a vehicle for the initiation of young people into sporting practices. Sport, on this view, is considered a socially significant and culturally valued aspect of contemporary society:

> sport, like science or medicine, is a particular type of human practice that has its own integrity and is governed and characterised by its own rules and ethos. Such practices are distinctive forms of activity worthwhile in life. (Arnold, 1992, p. 237)

Arnold develops the argument thus:

> sport…is a culturally valued practice that embodies some of human-kind's highest ideals and most cherished traditions. When sport is pursued for its own sake, its rules willingly followed, its finest conventions upheld, *sport becomes an ennobling and worthwhile form of life.* (1992, p. 239; emphasis added)

Thus, in the view of a number of contemporary PE academics worldwide, PE should focus upon initiation into the "rituals, values and traditions of a sport" (Siedentop, 1994, p. 7) as well as the skills of sport themselves. A growing list of publications in the PE subject-community appears to mark sport education out as an increasingly popular view of the purposes of PE (see, for example, Penney *et al.*, 2002).

It is noticeable that the views espoused by Alderson and

Crutchley (1990), Almond (1996) and others who have advocated the adoption of a sport education model for PE often portray it in far more utilitarian terms than (and are, therefore, somewhat at odds with) the purely intrinsic justification that Arnold (1992, 1997), as a philosopher, favours. It is interesting to observe how these seemingly extrinsically oriented views of sport education appear to incorporate more conventional, instrumental, views of PE typically associated with the academic or health ideologies. Almond, for example, is not content with what might be termed the "pure" or "restricted" conception of PE as an initiation into the valued cultural practice of sport through sport education. He appears to want not merely education *in* sport but to incorporate education *through* sport, in particular via the introduction of youngsters to "inter-personal competencies" through PE (1996, p. 194). In this regard, it is noteworthy that even Siedentop adds the caveat that he does not "advocate that physical education should be transformed totally into sport education" (1994, p. 6). He adds that sport education "is not meant to replace physical education" nor "reduce or eliminate attention to physical fitness, dance, leisure pursuits, and adventure education" (p. 6). Thus, in tune with Almond's view, Siedentop argues that sport education is "one part of the physical education programme". Nonetheless, for Siedentop, sport education involves more than "typical PE sport"; that is to say:

> students not only learn more completely how to play sports but also to co-ordinate and manage their sport experiences. They also learn individual responsibility and effective group membership skills. (Siedentop, 1994, p. 3)

This interpretation of sport education, when coupled with its avowed objectives (see Siedentop, 1994, pp. 4-5), creates a picture of an approach that appears to share two things with the health and academic ideologies, as well as NCPE: firstly, concern with more than merely the performance of sport; and, secondly, an associated concern for the utilisation of sport and physical activity to achieve broader educational goals, whether they relate to health or intellectual development.

Alexander, Taggart and Thorpe (1996), on the other hand, clearly do not view sport education as a compromise between intrinsically and extrinsically valued perspectives. They describe sport education as "curriculum *replacement* rather than repair" (p. 27; emphasis added) and refer to Sparkes's (1990) characterisation of "ideological change" of this kind, "involving lasting changes to the values, beliefs and commitments underpinning teachers' pedagogies" (p. 27). In the light of the seemingly profound influence of changing philosophical justifications for PE in the curriculum that sport education appears to represent, it is interesting to note Alexander *et al.*'s (1996) suggestion that sport education represents a political (and, thus, ideological) rather than a philosophical basis for the re-evaluation of the concept of PE. In this context, they see sport education as a response to the "failure" and "marginality" of PE in the school curriculum. They point to Locke's "admonition that replacing the dominant programme model was the only thing which could rescue secondary physical education from marginality and demise" (cited in Alexander *et al.*, 1996, p. 26). Alexander *et al.* summarise the position thus:

> if the profession was to deal with "disturbing levels of alienation, programme marginality in school curricula [and] deep and destructive role conflicts within those who teach"...then the change would have to be so deep...that it could only be referred to as curricular replacement rather than repair. (1996, p. 27)

It is clear, then, that the decade or so around the 1980s was not simply a period of changing ideologies. Continuities existed alongside the changes that were evidently taking place. Whilst the balance may have been shifting towards an ideology of health, the sporting ideology remained strong as variations on the theme began to emerge among academics and, to a lesser extent, teacher-trainers. This position of relative strength has been reinforced by a further sea change in the 1990s in the form of the introduction of the NCPE in 1992, followed by subsequent revisions in 1995 and 2000.

The Resurfacing of the Sporting Ideology

Several developments over the last decade or so have demonstrated that the sporting ideology, in one form or another, remains alive and well at various levels of the PE subject-community and within the public at large, as well as with other key players in the policy process, such as central Government. In 1995, the recently formed Department of National Heritage (DNH) published a policy statement — *Sport: Raising the game* — setting out the Government's intention to bring about "a sea-change in the prospects of British sport". Central to this was what was claimed to be the much-needed "renaissance" of sport in schools. The then Prime Minister, John Major, made clear his determination "to put sport back at the heart of weekly life in *every* school" (DNH, 1995, Foreword; emphasis in the original). *Raising the game* identified sport as the most significant element of the PE curriculum and identified an alleged need for extra sporting provision in schools. This overt attempt by the Conservative Government to provide a clear steer to PE was reiterated and underlined by the policy statement of the Labour Government that succeeded it. Entitled *A sporting future for all* (Department for Culture, Media and Sport[4] [DCMS], 2000) the policy focused particular attention upon extending the range of sporting opportunities available to youngsters after school (via extra-curricular PE), the creation of further specialist sports colleges and the enhancement of school links with community sports clubs.

Central to the policies of successive Conservative and Labour Governments has been the expectation that schools would provide more opportunities for sport within and beyond the curriculum and view extra-curricular sport as forming a more readily apparent *sporting* continuum with the formal PE curriculum. The emphasis upon sport and team games within the curriculum associated with the requirements of the 1995 revision of NCPE has not been substantially weakened or radically challenged by the 2000 revision nor by recent policy pronouncements of the Labour Government or Sport England. OFSTED and Her Majesty's Inspectorate (HMI) continue to be required, respectively, to survey the state of school sport in order to identify good practice and report annually on the state of PE and sport in schools. Teacher training is expected to involve student teachers in gaining more sporting qualifications and, in conjunction with this, increasing numbers of coaching courses are being made available to teachers. In addition, the rapid growth of "Sportsmark" awards for those schools meeting a minimum number of hours of extra-curricular sport and sports college status for those PE departments and schools deemed suitably sports-oriented and

---

[4] The Department for Culture, Media and Sport is the Labour Government's successor to the Conservative Government's Department of National Heritage.

qualified to act as focal points for the development of sport in their communities or regions confirms the continuing dominance of a sporting ideology at the political level. It is worthy of note, however, that successive Governments have evidently been of the opinion that their preferred view of PE (as virtually synonymous with sport) was, and continues to be, shared by the PE profession (or, at least, *teachers* of PE) — as witnessed by the then Prime Minister, John Major's, claim that "putting sport back at the heart of school life" was a "commitment…*shared…by the great majority of the teaching profession*" (DNH, 1996, Foreword; emphases added).

It also worthy of note that government pronouncements such as *Raising the game* (DNH, 1995, 1996) and *A sporting future for all* (DCMS, 2000) include a complex of intrinsic and extrinsic justifications for their preferred view of PE. Whilst their primary concern appears to be the repositioning of sport within PE, their justificatory comments lean more-or-less heavily on the academic (or "standard") justification for PE: intellectual (including moral) education through traditional team games and competitive sports. In addition to the more overt moral and political concerns of these policies — with character development as well as sporting excellence and international sporting success — there is clear evidence that messages about the contribution of PE to health promotion have filtered through to influence government policy towards PE. All this suggests that the current Labour administration will continue the pattern of implementing measures that will, in effect, constrain teachers to continue to orient PE towards sport, and particularly competitive team games, notwithstanding the recent "loosening" of the games emphasis at Key Stage 4 of the revised NCPE for 2000.

Conclusion

In this chapter I have sought to provide an outline of the ideological themes that, it is argued, have been more-or-less prominent within PE from the emergence of the subject in its nascent form, around the turn of the century, through to the established secondary school subject of the present day. On occasions (for example with HRE), it has been possible to identify connections, however tenuous or speculative, direct or indirect, between these ideological themes and academic philosophising about PE and the ideological discourse to be found in the subject-community. At times (for example with the sporting ideologies identified after WWII and then again in the 1990s) it is far more difficult to identify anything other than a tangential, one might say serendipitous, overlap between ideology and philosophy.

On the one hand, this is hardly surprising given that formal academic philosophising about PE did not develop as such until the late 1960s. On the other hand, however, it is noticeable that all of the ideologies in their contemporary incarnations make broadly philosophical claims – in the sense of being ostensibly underpinned by rational principles. Nevertheless, from a sociological perspective, these philosophies are more-or-less blatantly ideological by virtue of their tendencies to be more mythical and idealistic and less internally coherent than labelling them "philosophical" would suggest.

In Chapter 4, I intend to explore the views and perceptions of PE teachers as a forerunner to establishing, in Chapter 5, the extent to which their "philosophies" are suffused with ideological orientations whilst, at the same time, examining the relationship between these ideologies and teachers' predispositions and social contexts.

4

Physical Education Teachers on Physical Education

This chapter summarises and illustrates the findings from my recent study of PE teachers' aphoristic, or everyday, views on the nature and purposes of their subject. In doing so, it picks out the main ideological themes to be found within their "philosophies". In the first instance, however, it is worth referring to one particularly prominent leitmotif of teachers' responses: namely, the emphasis they tended to place on "enjoyment".

Enjoyment

In almost all responses to the question "What do you think PE should be about?" the word "enjoyment" featured prominently and, for the most part, explicitly. Enjoyment was a primary consideration for the teachers in the study. It tended to be the first thing they mentioned and was something they returned to time and time again: "[PE] should be about fun, it should be about engaging pupils". Typically, enjoyment formed an initial and immediate response, upon which teachers then elaborated. The emphasis upon enjoyment is worthy of note for several reasons. Firstly, enjoyment as such is not commonly offered as a goal of education. Indeed, one could not imagine teachers of academic subjects such as mathematics or history placing quite the same emphasis upon enjoyment. On the contrary, one would expect to find little sympathy amongst educationalists for enjoyment as an educational goal, for what is education, one might add, if not the antithesis of "fun"? Secondly, the emphasis upon enjoyment suggests that even teachers of PE perceived their subject as somehow "less serious" than other subjects. The teachers appeared to have a distinctive view of their own subject, implying that PE was not only a less serious subject but also that it was not really "educational" in the academic sense of the term. In this vein, some teachers viewed enjoyment as being an end in itself:

...some sort of success and enjoyment. Success might just mean enjoyment...to me that's as good as being an Olympic champion.

Frequently, however, enjoyment was justified on the basis of the *cathartic* role PE is commonly supposed to perform: that is to say, as a release from the intellectual demands being made on the children during the remainder of the school curriculum. In this sense, PE appeared to be seen by teachers as not so much a part of the academic content of education as a *release from* the academic aspects of school:

I think, essentially, it should be about enjoyment...getting children to do something physical — because in school they're just sitting down and working.

Indeed, some teachers appeared to view PE "as nothing more than a physical interlude to the more serious business of academic subjects" (Brooker, Kirk, Braiuka and Bransgrove, 2000, p. 14):

It's my job to get them active, release a bit of tension, get some energy out of their systems so they are ready for the rest of the school day. And one of the main priorities is that they enjoy themselves.

Thus, whilst for some teachers enjoyment was spoken of as an end in itself, more typically enjoyment was seen either as a *precondition* and/or a *vehicle* for other outcomes: that is to say, enjoyment was seen as necessary as well as desirable. It was deemed necessary for *pragmatic* reasons (for example, class management) and desirable for *"philosophical"* reasons. For purely pragmatic reasons some teachers felt the need to veer towards enjoyment in the lesson as a vehicle for greater control over the pupils:

One of the things would be enjoyment — otherwise you've got a problem straight away, you know, if they won't do it.

control...if somebody is not happy with doing something...they're not likely to turn round and say, "Well, it's good this!" If I allow them to play the game in a constructive manner and they feel as if they're doing something...that's positive and that will work — the control will be much better.

The head of department (HoD) who provided the latter comment, also observed that this was not the way he had taught before, nor the way he wanted to teach. He added, "It's just so very foreign to me. It's a totally different way of doing things for me". He concluded,

> So, it's a bit of give and take. I've still got my "skill development" and they [the pupils] have got what they perceived was theirs [the fun element]. So, rather than have the confrontation all the time...

Interestingly, this HoD appeared acutely aware that this kind of pragmatic "trade-off", in the form of an implicit negotiation with the pupils, might appear as some kind of betrayal of the process of teaching "traditional" PE to other teachers. He added,

> I think people would view what I did this year [as] perhaps either a "kop-out" or negative, not "traditional" PE...you know...you can see a few people saying that.

It is also interesting to note that being aware of (one might say, inter-dependent with) the "generalized other" — in the form of an imaginary stereotypical PE teacher — appeared to have a bearing on this teacher's view of what he was doing. He felt uneasy having to "trade off" his perception of an ideal-type PE lesson with the constraints of the situation as he perceived them.

Not only was enjoyment a vehicle for achieving classroom management objectives, for many teachers enjoyment was an *aid to the process of learning* the requisite physical skills and personal habits that they also took to be a feature of PE:

> As long as they are getting stuck in to whatever they are doing, and they come off [having worked up] a bit of a sweat and they have enjoyed it...they will almost certainly learn something from the lesson as well... They have got to learn more if they are enjoying it. They will come looking forward to the lesson. They're going to make more of an effort and be more receptive to what you do.

> I think if they are enjoying things they...will have a go at things. In the gym, for example, if you can make gym lessons a bit more lively and entertaining you'll get kids losing that sense of fear...it is just a way of doing the activity in the most productive way, really. If you can get them really involved and enjoying it then they will get more out of it, and they'll take more "on board" as well. They will listen more to what you've got to say and they will see that it leads to an end product which they are going to like.

Once again, the views of teachers of PE appear particularly interesting when considered alongside other subjects on the secondary-school curriculum. One wonders whether enjoyment is generally seen as necessary (rather than merely desirable) to the process of learning, for example, English grammar, algebra, geography or history.

One HoD articulated her conception of the developmental nature of the learning process in PE and the manner in which *enjoyment*, classroom *control* and *learning* were frequently associated (explicitly and implicitly) with each other in teachers' minds:

> I think it's enjoyment...what we offer the pupils is for them to enjoy the lesson and make sure that we cater for everybody... If the pupils don't enjoy the lessons...then how are you going to keep them [interested] and so on? Once you have got the fun side and you have got them enjoying the lessons then you can start to educate them in all the other aspects...the social co-operation of teamwork, individual skill levels. You have definitely got to have that enjoyment [in] taking part in the lesson before they can begin to learn.

It was clear that enjoyment and learning were linked in a variety of ways in many teachers' thinking:

> If pupils don't enjoy it they won't learn and so...I don't think we'd get much done.

> Well, if they are not enjoying it they are going to switch off...I mean, how are you going to get enjoyment from those who hate going out on a hockey pitch; which you can appreciate when they haven't got the co-ordination and perhaps never will have. And they get to really hate PE...[so] why not do something...they really enjoy?

To many teachers in the study, enjoyment was also seen as a vehicle for the development of the kind of *active lifestyles* that would promote health by developing adherence to activity in a manner that would be likely to persist beyond school and into later life:

> I like to think they would go away from my lesson and go and do [physical activity] out of school hours. And if they don't enjoy it in school they are not going to want to do it outside of school...I wouldn't be a PE teacher if I didn't think they should try and be fit and healthy.

Enjoyment was, then, frequently presented as a vehicle for achieving "philosophical" or rather, sociologically speaking, ideological goals — particularly *adherence to sport and physical activity*. As such, enjoyment was seen as a precondition in many teachers' eyes for the encouragement of ongoing participation, and thus healthy lifestyles:

> I think that if we can introduce the children to even just one activity that

> they'd like to do out of school... Because if they don't enjoy it...they won't do it again. They have *got* to enjoy it [emphasis in the original].

Thus, teachers were particularly keen to encourage adherence to physical activity and sport via the medium of enjoyment:

> They [should] come out of school and have a go at playing...when they leave school. To say, "Well, I really enjoyed that sport and I want to carry on after school"...that is something we have achieved.

Enjoyment was also viewed as a vehicle for the development of confidence amongst all pupils — but particularly among girls — as a stepping stone to participation.

Thus, enjoyment was at the heart of the "philosophies" of teachers in this study. Enjoyment was seen as the key to *control*, to *learning* and, above all, to *participation*. In short, if pupils enjoyed PE then pretty much everything else might reasonably be expected to follow: pupils were seen as more likely to do PE and sport now and in the future. And the latter mattered to these teachers. For, in various ways, the teachers expressed a clear desire to bring about an adherence, on the part of their pupils, to physical activity and sport, an adherence that was likely to endure in the form of a lifelong commitment to participation with the associated benefits for health. And yet, despite this preoccupation with enjoyment in teachers' thinking, it is noticeable, as one teacher observed, that enjoyment as a term does not feature in the NCPE:

> I think one thing that is disappointing about this PE National Curriculum is that it doesn't mention the word "enjoyment" anywhere...when kids...come to PE lessons I think there should be an enjoyment element to it. I don't for one minute say that it should be all play, but they should be encouraged to enjoy what's going on...I think it's a key aim, it's one of the main key aims.

One wonders whether viewing enjoyment as a precondition for the achievement of "philosophical" — or, more exactly, educational — goals is anything more than a rationalization for the fact that "fun" would not be seen as a sufficient justification for a school subject. Indeed, it often seemed the case that "philosophical" justifications were presented as afterthoughts — "add-ons" intended to make the pragmatic reasons more palatable. This is a significant point and one to which I will return later on in the book.

It is clear that, when set alongside the relatively prescriptive demands of the National Curriculum as a whole, teachers of PE appeared to view their subject as in some ways "special" and "different" from other subjects, not least in terms of their emphasis upon enjoyment as "a key aim" of PE. This discrepancy between the relatively more academic "philosophy" behind the NCPE and teachers' everyday "philosophies" is quite revealing in so far as it is indicative of some of the problems associated with a justification for a National Curriculum in PE that bears little trace of the practical concerns and realities of teachers' day-to-day lives. Whatever the underpinning ideology for PE teachers' "philosophies" and practice, enjoyment of PE was seen as a necessary prerequisite. This was the case, particularly, for those who subscribed to "education for leisure", "sport for all" and health ideologies.

This raises several important questions: Are PE teachers justified in assuming that education should be "fun"? What would OFSTED or, for that matter, Her Majesty's Chief Inspector of Schools have to say about such claims? Of equal significance for the theme of this book, what would academic philosophers of education have to say about this justification? Characterisations of teaching and learning in the academic literature (such as that of Oakeshott, 1972) incorporate many things but nowhere is mention made of "fun" — explicitly or implicitly — as a defining feature of either.

Before exploring the ideology of health as a prominent ideological justification for PE in the eyes of PE teachers, it is worth noting the links or continuities between justifications. This is especially so with reference to the link between fun/enjoyment, "education for leisure", "sport for all" and concerns about health, as illustrated in the following teachers' comments:

> I believe that [the] main function of a PE teacher, or PE department, is to introduce the pupils to physical activity — health — so that in the long term, when they leave school, they continue to take part in some sort of physical activity. And in the short term, while they are at school, they learn social skills and they learn how to enjoy themselves.

> Basically [it's] about offering pupils the opportunity to compete in a lot of sports so that they can…keep healthy…so that once they have finished school they don't just become sort of "couch potatoes" and hopefully…find something they like and carry on outside of school.

The sometimes explicit, sometimes implicit, links between various justifications reflected the common occurrence of a union of diverse elements within teachers' "philosophies". Prominent amongst such amalgam "philosophies" was the theme of health.

The Ideology of Health

Health Promotion through PE

Alongside their ostensible concern with enjoyment, PE teachers were keen to express a desire to encourage active, "healthy" lifestyles. As one might have expected, given the pre-eminence of an ideology of health in recent years (Colquhoun, 1991; Green, 1994), many teachers appeared to view health as *the* current issue confronting PE teachers:

> The health side of it is more and more important…the health and participation part [of PE]…and getting them to realise why they're doing it and why it's important…with regard to what it's actually doing within your body…an awareness of the health aspect.

> Quite a big thing is made about the health side of things…I see it as important. It affects the nation basically. It affects me because…I have to pay for people who are unwell…if we can cut down the costs of the NHS etc. etc. then that will all have benefits [for] everybody.

For some, health had even come to overshadow "traditional" PE — with its emphasis on team games — as the contemporary *raison d'être* for PE:

> We teach netball, hockey…bringing in all your motor skills and that's important, as is the team aspect, but to me the health-related [aspect] is more important.

Thus, for many teachers, health promotion was considered either implicitly or explicitly to be *the* function of PE:

> I think it's *our duty* really that children should be as active as possible and, obviously, we're trying to encourage children to become more involved in sport, in *later* life, and so we introduce them to sports — so that they…have a lot of enjoyment in later life, socially [emphasis added].

> Because we've got the vehicle for it [health promotion], really; that we can try to promote this to children: the way to stay healthy, the way to a healthy lifestyle, things like that.

It is quite revealing and informative that, without having mastered the details or, indeed, the precise implications for their practice, PE teachers have a general idea that PE—frequently in the form of sport—"does children good".

A recurring theme of this book is recognition of the fact that teachers' "philosophies" are not especially likely to have been formed by professional, let alone academic, writing on the subject. Some teachers did make reference to developments that they perceived as occurring "as a result of documents coming out" as well as "research in a lot of PE articles". More often, however, the emphasis placed upon health was not perceived by the teachers themselves as having developed in response to the "call to arms" to be found in the academic press and frequently espoused by academics and teacher-trainers themselves. PE teachers' views were more likely to refer to the effect of "newspapers; your own belief…[there's] so much more in the news".

PE Teachers' Common-Sense Assumptions Regarding the Fitness of Young People

For many teachers in the study, health promotion as a, even *the*, justification for PE was intimately related to a taken-for-granted conviction that children and young people are less "fit" than they were.[1] Indeed, as Harris (1994b) has observed, the term "fitness" was often used by teachers as if it were viewed as synonymous with health:

> the level of fitness [among youngsters] is so much poorer than years ago. And that is a legacy of the fact that the PE departments aren't doing their jobs…the pupils are less fit, the pupils don't run any more, or don't run enough within their physical education lessons, so the heart rate never goes up to a level that will get many fit. And, unfortunately, that's how it's going.

In this vein, the views of teachers in this study appeared to add weight to Roberts's (1995, 1996a, 1996b, 1997) claims that they have, since the 1970s, become increasingly aware of constraints towards sedentariness in many areas of young people's lives. At the same time, however, it was noticeable that teachers did frequently appear unaware of the growing popularity of sport and physical activity

---

[1] A belief which, as several authors (see, for example, Armstrong, McManus, Welsman and Kirby, 1996; Armstrong, Welsman and Kirby, 1998) have pointed out, is by no means necessarily accurate.

among young people (Roberts, 1996a). It was commonplace for teachers to allege slothfulness among "[the] young people of today":

> Nowadays there's so many people that just don't seem to do any physical activity; it's more behind desks, or at the computer. I think…it's getting more and more so that they need to get out and be active and realise the importance of being active… We are always talking to them about the importance of doing some kind of activity… We always talk about why we should be doing it — exercise — as much as possible and as often as possible…to get as much activity as we can out of them [in] the timetable, then offer them lots of extra-curricular clubs that they can come and take part in.

Thus, frequently associated with teachers' taken-for-granted views regarding the levels of inactivity as well as the alleged lack of fitness among youngsters were beliefs that modern lifestyles were largely associated with declining levels of activity:

> I can guarantee that out of a class of 30 you would have a lot of struggling kids of the same age, whereas 20 years ago people were that much more [active], they could cope with anything like that a lot better…I think the natural fitness of children is not what it was; they are ferried about from place to place.

The Relationship between Sport, Fitness and Health

For many PE teachers who subscribed, more or less, to a health ideology, sport was still seen as the main vehicle for health promotion:

> My view of PE is that, on the very basic level, I'm here to improve fitness, strength and promote health with all the kids…my fundamental job is to raise levels of fitness and skill expertise in whatever area I'm working in…*we're talking about why we need sport*, what they will get out of it as an individual, as a purely health-related thing, and how we want them to go on and be involved in sport for the rest of their lives [emphasis added].

Thus, the comments of a significant proportion of the teachers in this study, regarding the role of PE in health promotion, bore the traces of what might justifiably be referred to as a preoccupation with sport in the interests of both the physical and mental health of the individual:

> I feel sport has a role to play on that…fitness side of things… And, again, it's the social side…if you're committed to a sport and you are 14 or 15, you are far less likely to get involved with street-corner gangs, far less likely to get involved with drugs and that side of

things...so it has a lot of good things that stop pupils getting involved with things that perhaps they shouldn't.

Some teachers highlighted what they saw as the importance of the health of the nation as well as the health of the individual:

I think in general what it should offer is for pupils of all abilities to take part in some form of physical education... [The] first reason I'll give is obviously the health of the nation, basically, and the health of the individual. A lot of kids nowadays...are using...things, other than sport, for their enjoyment in pastimes... What we can do is try and offer a variety of sports so that somebody somewhere finds a sport they are interested in.

HRE Programmes in Practice

Where HRE featured in PE teachers' purported practice it did so, for the most part, "in a block of work", typically of several weeks duration, and was more usually referred to as health-related *fitness* (HRF) rather than as health-related *exercise* (HRE) — the term preferred in contemporary professional and academic writing (Harris, 1994a). Frequently, HRE took the form of variations on the theme of "circuits". One teacher said, "It's only been more recently that I have taught health and fitness and that's just been circuits and going on a run". This is a format which, in line with Harris's (1994b) observation, persists despite various teachers' comments that it is something "the kids don't particularly like". However, in teachers' eyes, whether or not circuits appeared attractive to the pupils was also dependent, at least in part, upon the resources available:

It depends on your facilities; if you've got state-of-the-art exercise equipment then it [HRE] can be quite interesting...but [here] it's quite a limited experience...[regarding] what you can actually do.

For a number of years now, the NCPE has stipulated that HRE should be a permeating theme in PE programmes. This requirement for permeation does not appear to have left its mark on many PE teachers' thinking, let alone their practice. Various teachers "delivered [HRF] as a 'block' shared with orienteering". The nature of many teachers' comments was such that it suggested that "health" provides a convenient justificatory ideology, which was latched on to by teachers more often for reasons of pragmatism rather than because it had been systematically thought through and implemented in the curriculum. When asked if she managed to tease out or emphasise HRE as a permeating theme in compliance with NCPE, one teacher responded for many when she commented, "Not sure, really". Despite this, many teachers expressed the view that the "health" theme permeated their work as a matter of course:

> I don't focus on it in the sense that I don't say, "Well…this area is where we are going to hit health"… But to me *it's something that is always there when we do any activity* [emphasis added].

There was, it was claimed, what amounted to a kind of de facto permeation:

> We don't do specific units on health-related fitness. We do do some work within the GCSE on health-related fitness but no specific unit as such. When we do things like aerobics it's definitely associated with health-related fitness. Swimming also, I would say.

It is worth noting that this was a feature of many teachers' responses to several questions of this kind. They appeared not to have thought very much, if at all, about whether some aspect or other of their "philosophies" (such as character building, moral development, health promotion) actually took place or not; they simply assumed, or took it for granted, that it did. In this regard, their thinking appeared rich with fantasy inasmuch as they were keen to defend what might be seen as a somewhat romanticised view of the achievements of PE, despite being unable to identify the whereabouts of some of the claimed features in their own teaching and not having identified these features in their initial "philosophies".

Notwithstanding the extent to which they perceived HRE as permeating their everyday practice of PE, various teachers viewed their roles as providing pupils with "direct information" about health in the belief that this could be expected to have an impact upon their behaviour. Such a view is consistent with Colquhoun's (1991) claim that an "ideology of health" prevails in PE, focusing attention upon, and responsibility for, individuals' health and wellbeing on the individuals themselves rather than their context and circumstances. Teachers tended to view PE as having prime responsibility for increasing knowledge and understanding of what many believe to be the straightforward relationship between exercise, health promotion and the fostering of enthusiasm for physical activity.

A health ideology appears, then, to have risen to occupy a

prominent place on the ideological high ground of PE teachers' "philosophies" over the last decade or so. In line with the kinds of views expressed by PE teachers in the recent studies of Mason (1995) and Sport England (2001), traces of a health ideology were more or less apparent in virtually all teachers' comments in the present study. Despite this, one is left with the clear impression that, whilst PE teachers are broadly aware of the requirements of NCPE in relation to health and HRE, this remains a rather vague awareness, both of the rationale for HRE and of the manner in which it is required to be implemented according to NCPE.

HRE and "Education for Leisure"

Roberts (1995, pp. 339-340) noted that in Mason's (1995) research on behalf of the Sports Council:

> teachers defended their broad curricula as the best way of maximising the number of pupils who find a sport at which they are competent and which they enjoyed, and which would extend their participation into their out-of-school and post-school lives.

Roberts (1996a) identified several trends that have led to the higher levels of participation by young people in sport in the 1990s and to the marked decline in the dropout rate during late adolescence in recent years. Prominent amongst these trends was the adoption by "virtually all schools" in the 1980s of "sport for all" policies together with the broadening of sports curricula. From the 1970s and into the 1980s, "the sports interests of young people were steadily broadening both within the physical education curriculum and outside school time" (Houlihan, 1991, p. 226) as the traditional games-based PE curricula were significantly modified by teachers, not least in terms of the provision of "options" – or, as OFSTED (1998) refer to it, "activity choice"[2] – for upper-school youngsters as part of the trend towards "education for [post-school] leisure" (Scraton, 1992). Roberts's (1995, 1996a) observation – that many teachers in the 1970s and 1980s had broadened the PE curricula they offered, not only by adding activities to the traditional diet but also by offering an element of choice – was borne out by teachers in this study. For many teachers, the way to bring about adherence to sport and physical activity was considered to be through "option" PE. Thus,

[2] The terms will be used interchangeably.

increasingly associated with the health ideology (chronologically and conceptually) have been the relatively more marginal, but nevertheless complementary, ideologies of "education for leisure" and "sport for all".

The "Education for Leisure" Ideology

According to Roberts (1996a, 1996b) and Scraton (1992), since the 1970s teachers have been increasingly aware of, and have responded to, wider social trends regarding developments in youth culture. This appeared to be borne out by the comments of a number of teachers:

> there's so many other things around now that we have to compete with...which are offering...adrenaline rushes...So, I think we have to try and say, "Yes, we can achieve a high and an adrenaline rush from sports, as well as those other things, but on top of that we can offer you extra things and relationships of belonging, of physical wellbeing".

Consistent with the claims of Roberts and Scraton, a variety of teachers in this study perceived PE as competing with alternative attractions:

> It's [PE] about...participation...hopefully...that they try, that they want to do something outside...in sport, in activities, in being active rather than sitting around and watching television, you know... To me, PE encompasses a lot of things, it's not just one major factor, it's got a lot of things to offer individuals...yes – enjoyment, participation.

Such comments seem to offer support for Roberts's (1996b) claim that one of the reasons that PE has, over the last decade or so, been what he terms "a success story" in participatory terms, is that PE teachers have been "in tune" with young people's changing leisure lifestyles and circumstances. Teachers' responses suggested, also, that they were aware of the desirability of encouraging enjoyment and competence in a breadth of sports. Roberts and Brodie (1992) have referred to this as the desirability of "a wide sporting repertoire" on the part of young people. This was expressed by teachers in the following terms:

> so that when they become adults...they would have experienced and enjoyed a cross-section of sports, so that they are...capable [enough] to go on and say, "Yes, I enjoyed that, I want to keep that going...I know where I can go", and they can carry on playing.

Once again, it was noticeable that teachers frequently assumed that this continuing participation would be achieved through sport and sports clubs:

> I'm looking for when they leave school, [that they] continue…some form of physical activity…they've got enjoyment [from PE] in school…[and] want some form of activity to ensure they are healthy when they leave. That's my prime aim, I would say.

Mason (1995) described similar responses in her study, in terms of PE teachers' embracing the mass participation ethos associated with the Sports Council's "sport for all" policy. In similar vein, many teachers in the present study expressed a desire to encourage all pupils to acquire a commitment to physical activity in general and sport in particular.

The "Sport for All" Ideology

"Sport for all" appeared frequently, often prominently, in the justifications of many PE teachers in this study, both explicitly — as a phrase utilised by teachers to explain their policies — and implicitly, as a theme recognisable in a range of viewpoints:

> My job is to cater for everybody in my school with various sports.

"Sport for All" and Schools in Disadvantaged Areas

Interestingly, "sport for all" was a "philosophy" particularly common among those teaching in disadvantaged[3] areas. Teachers in such schools frequently introduced or qualified their statements with references to "*this* school", or this "*type* of area" and even "*these* kids":

> Well, what I've tried over the years, basically, in *this* school, was to give kids an opportunity in any sports… My job is to try to cater for everybody in my school with various sports, to the extent that now we can teach golf, archery, bowls. Because, I think there are some chubby lads…who perhaps don't like doing a lot of running and things like that but would really get a lot out of some of the other sorts of sport. I think that's my role in life, to give them a taste [of sport] and hopefully

---

[3] As indicated by the proportion of pupils entitled to free school meals at the school.

> they will take it from there and so develop their own interests [emphasis added].

Various teachers, working in relatively disadvantaged schools, proffered views similar to those of one HoD:

> In this country, the only opportunity some kids get for sport is within school...the vast majority of working-class children get their first opportunity within schools... As a PE teacher it's got to be "sport for all".

It was noticeable, then, that the comments of a number of PE teachers —especially those teaching in disadvantaged areas—included specific references to the "types" of pupils in a manner that suggested that their views on PE incorporated degrees of what might be termed "localism". In referring to what they perceived as a need to adapt their aims, expectations and practices to the "types" of pupils they taught, these teachers demonstrated a tendency towards degrees of adaptation to programmes that one would not expect to find in other (more academic) National Curriculum subjects. Indeed, the *National* Curriculum does not cater for such qualifications according to the "character" or location of the school. Nor, it is worth reminding ourselves, do the philosophies articulated by academic philosophers of PE allow for — let alone expect — degrees of localism in their justifications for the subject.

"Sport for All" and Girls

"Sport for all" was a particularly prominent "philosophy" where teachers felt themselves compelled to adapt to what they saw as the particular constraints of teaching PE to girls:

> While they're in school I want to teach them these skills and hope that it transfers to later on in life...we find that some...particularly Year 11 girls, if they don't want to do [PE] they will not. They will sit on the side line, even if they have their PE kit there! If they don't like sports they won't do it. So, at one point two terms ago, we gave them a choice of three things they could do.

In this regard, teachers (and especially female teachers) appeared particularly concerned with girls' health and fitness:

> In the last two or three years we've seen an increase, especially in the girls...not wanting to do it. And the reason they don't want to do it is because they are unfit and overweight.

> [For girls] I'd drop athletics...I'd do it a lot more as health-related, fitness orientated... Why are we making them run around the track three and three-quarter times? They walk it...and that is a way of putting them off...there [are] better ways of getting them interested in getting fit.

Whilst concern about the impact of gender, particularly on girls, was expressed for the most part by female teachers, it was not confined to them. A young male PE teacher commented:

> Teacher: We do a lot of gymnastics lower down and then we move more [towards] individual [activities] in terms of aerobics and trampolining as they go up [the school].
> KG: Why?
> Teacher: Because of body shape changes and...[to offer activities] they may want to take up later on in life.

It was apparent, then, that various teachers' comments could be interpreted as exemplifying "education for leisure" or "sport for all" ideologies; for example: "if you do this, you'll thank me in five years time!" Insofar as such "philosophies" were often linked with "option" PE, they suggested that what the teachers *thought* was usually related to what they had come to believe on the basis of *experience*: that their dispositions towards PE had altered as their networks encompassed pupils and schools in disadvantaged areas and this, in various ways, came to constrain their practice of PE.

"Activity Choice" or "Option" PE

A particular feature of teachers' "philosophies" and practice that appeared somewhat idiosyncratic (especially in relation to the expectations and practices of teachers of other curricula subjects) was their commitment to "option" PE. Despite the fact that the scope for offering choice has been very much limited by the NCPE, it was nevertheless particularly noticeable that many teachers remained committed to it and managed to squeeze "choice" in as, in effect, a continuation of what might be called their "pre-NCPE" practice:

> I always have done ["option"] PE...only in Key Stage 4...to give them a wider base... There were more options available than there were teachers to teach it [a continuation of pre-NCPE practice].

Many teachers would have liked to be able to offer a wider range of options:

> I think we should give them a broader range of experiences and give them as many opportunities as we can to do as many different things...they might be really good at something.

For many teachers, choice or "options" was viewed as an essential "tool of the trade":

> We introduce things like the minority sports... I think it's very important at Year 9 to introduce these other sports to them.

> ...getting [pupils] a bit more choice...we do try and give them as broad a range as possible.

As committed to "activity choice" as they appeared in principle, many teachers, nevertheless, still viewed it as following on (chronologically and developmentally) from skill development. They saw the early years of secondary PE (Years 7, 8 and 9: Key Stage 3) as focusing upon teaching "the basics": in other words, the acquisition of "key" sporting (but also physical) skills that would, in their view, allow a more "recreational", leisure-oriented emphasis in Key Stage 4 (years 10 and 11):

> I suppose in Key Stage 3 we offer a more narrow curriculum in the more traditional type activities...developing their skill... Then, perhaps in Key Stage 4, we'd give them a wider choice of activities — things like they could take up when they leave school, things like that...to give them the opportunity to experience what there is available.

> First, second and third year [Years 7, 8 and 9], they do netball, hockey, gym and dance — very traditional, very middle-of-the road type of things. Whereas [Years 10 and 11]...they go to the multi-gym, which is something they could actually go and do themselves. They get to have a go at badminton...I think it is seen as more *recreation*...let them just go and play, just go and do it [emphasis added].

In light of high-profile concerns of the 1980s alluded to by Evans (1990), regarding the dangers of so-called "progressive" PE, it is worthy of note that much of what passes as "activity choice" in the PE curriculum could not adequately be construed as "revolutionary"; that is to say, it does not involve discarding what might be seen as the "traditional" (sport- and team-game-oriented) PE curriculum.

Moreover, it seems to bear out Roberts's (1996a, 1996b) observations that the "options" made available to pupils *supplemented* rather than *replaced* "traditional" PE. It was noticeable, nonetheless, that the choice of activities was far more likely to be of additional sports rather than physical recreation activities as such:

> We do a little bit [of optional choice] but it's more…"traditional"; you either play hockey, netball, football — very traditional sport. And, again, you are teaching them a specific skill.

> As a department, we value all aspects; but we realise where our strengths lie [games]…[and] by giving more time to games you could introduce more games.

This was the case even though many of the teachers in this study were acutely aware that the staple PE diet — of sport and particularly team games — was not popular with many children:

> A lot of them are intimidated by games.

> That…can be off-putting to some children if they are made to do something they really don't enjoy.

It is noticeable that the justification for offering "choice" frequently returned to the aim of finding something that pupils *enjoyed* rather than developing new skills, a wider sporting repertoire or even in terms of other specifically educational objectives. Having said that, "activity choice" in PE was perceived by many teachers as a catalyst for encouraging the kinds of enjoyment and commitment likely to lead to longer-term adherence to physical activity and, thus, "healthy" lifestyles:

> that's a way…of getting into [sport] — if you [talk] about enjoyment and health for life — that's going to be the pathway to get that…child to enjoy health for life. It's a happy medium isn't it between pushing them to do something and realising…[that] if you bring something that they really enjoy…that is going to help them in later life, for the rest of their lives, much more than having this image of something they really hated and [will] never touch again.

Frequently, teachers commented to the effect that, in their experience, offering pupils an element of choice of activities had a positive effect on participation rates — especially with older pupils and girls ("the participation rate was brilliant…our participation rate, our enjoyment rate, the success of the kids"). Once again, this was particularly the case in schools located in relatively deprived social areas. It appears somewhat ironic, then, that OFSTED, in its 1998 report, claimed that a "move away from the 'recreational activities' and 'activity choice' approach is also raising achievement levels in Key Stage 4" (OFSTED, 1998, p. 1). This is a particularly interesting development, for it suggests, quite clearly, that, whereas PE teachers' goals are often couched in terms of "enjoyment", the goals of OFSTED remain phrased in terms of "achievement levels". OFSTED emphasises the *educational* objectives of PE and appears to be trying to move PE towards mainstream educational goals and formally defined criteria, which they, and others, can measure in a form that will stand up to public scrutiny. One might reasonably speculate that for OFSTED (and very probably for the general public), for example, enjoyment would not stand up to scrutiny as an objective for PE.

It would seem from teachers' comments that the development away from "activity choice" — forced upon teachers by the demands of NCPE as well as the expectations of OFSTED — has not met with universal approval. Indeed, a number of teachers commented that they would like greater scope at Key Stage 4 to choose what activities to offer children, ostensibly in order that pupils themselves might retain a degree of choice. Several teachers commented in negative terms about advice from inspectors to narrow their provision down in order to improve standards. One teacher's comments were illustrative of the manner in which various teachers favoured "activity choice" in PE, in part, for pragmatic reasons. These teachers perceived a need to adapt their practice to the constraints of the area and children at their schools. Commenting upon how he would have liked to plan the PE curriculum on reflection and after negotiation (with the pupils and even the parents) before then deciding on content and delivery, he said:

> Ideally, I would like to sit back and wait for the timetable and then look at the area and then look at the pupils and...[get the views of the parents and the children].

Other comments suggested a desire among teachers to be more adaptable to "tastes" and opportunities than they were, in practice, constrained to be:

> We always sit there and say, "Well, it would be great to get the kids out of school, go off with them, with sports they could do when they leave school"... We offer them quite a limited [range] of all the sports that are available.

Nonetheless, and in tune with Roberts's (1995, 1996a, 1996b) comments regarding the threat to NCPE posed by teachers' attempts to adapt the PE curriculum to correspond with contemporary youth cultures, various teachers commented upon the allegedly built-in limitations of NCPE:

> I don't think...school offer[s]...what children can do when they leave school or...what's provided in the community.

At the same time, and as indicated earlier, it was not uncommon for teachers to have a mistaken appreciation of trends in participation:

> Netball is...extremely popular... Outside of school, it's the most participated in sport for females.

A gender dimension was again evident. The comments of a number of female teachers, in particular, suggested that incorporating "activity choice" was perceived as a far more pressing matter for girls than for boys:

> It's much easier for boys to take up sport than it is for girls.

> Yesterday I gave a class a choice [for] the last lesson and I said right you've got the sports hall what would you like to do. Half put their hands up for netball and half of them just ducked their heads because the half that put their hands up for netball are the school team and love it and the other ones just didn't want to know...because they don't like sport they don't want to get involved...a lot of people who bring these notes in are the ones that don't enjoy [PE].

Specialisation on a limited number of activities (as per NCPE) and the re-emphasis upon traditional team games, frequently encouraged by OFSTED in their reports to the schools in this study, appeared both unpopular and was frequently viewed by teachers as potentially counterproductive. One teacher commented that:

> It has changed with Years 10 and 11 quite dramatically because we used to do a lot of activities to try and find activities for the children to do, enjoy and participate [in] for the rest of their lives, but we had an inspection. An inspector came in and criticised us for not...concentrating enough on specialist activities for Years 10 and 11, so we've narrowed it down. We now give a much greater [emphasis to] skills and time to specialist activities.

He added:

> I'm still quite critical about that, I don't think it's right. I think some children are missing out now on activities which we can't fit in. I find

> Years 10 and 11 would prefer a broader base... So, I think it's far too narrow. I would like them to have the opportunity to do things like volleyball and badminton; especially for the children that don't like the football and basketball. But we were actually told we should narrow it down after the OFSTED [inspection].

With this clear tension between many teachers' preference for "activity choice" and the constraints imposed by NCPE and the OFSTED inspection process in mind, it is worth reminding ourselves of Roberts's (1996a, 1996b) comments. Roberts argues that in broadening the curricula PE teachers had been succeeding at "moving with the flow" of "the broader tides" in young people's preferred uses of leisure, and that policies set on re-emphasising sport and team games (such as those recommended in *Sport: Raising the game* [DNH, 1995], *A sporting future for all* [DCMS, 2000] and apparently prevalent in OFSTED inspection advice to PE teachers) are likely to undo much of what he sees as the good work achieved in participatory terms over the last 20 years.

As previously intimated, with regard to teachers' adaptation of their practices and "philosophies" in accordance with the school contexts in which they operated, it was interesting to note that many teachers also identified a process of change in their "philosophies" towards "activity choice" associated with the "type" of pupils and "kinds" of schools they found themselves teaching in:

> My views had started to be shaped [by the socio-economic area]... I started to put into practice [options]...we did what the pupils wanted and they could get a benefit from.

As if to emphasise the way in which recent developments had worked to limit his attempts to broaden the curriculum, this teacher added:

> I've not been able to do that here because of the National Curriculum, because I've been OFSTEDed in my first year. And we're being OFSTEDed again in November. So, I've got to make sure my department [know] what the guidelines under the National Curriculum say. [We're] doing what the school expects, having everything planned out.

Finally, however, a caveat should be added, lest one were to form the impression that "option" PE is one area in which there *is* a consensus among PE teachers. Not all teachers were converts to "activity choice":

> It might look good, to some extent, "Oh yes, we're making use of our sports centre, we're going there and we're doing weights and we're doing swimming and we're doing this", but it's all *leisure* and when the boy gets puffed out he stops!...*the idea of fun and leisure at the moment is mediocrity.* Fun can be about achievement. Why is it that we don't push anymore? Why is it that we're prepared to accept poor standards in behaviour and discipline. I'll tell you what's prevalent now in children of the 90s: "I don't want to do this anymore and my mum says it's OK!"...*my job is to promote sport at every level* [emphases added].

Whilst "activity choice" appeared to have been embraced by very many of the teachers in this study, there were those who held out for a more traditional curriculum. They were more likely than not to be established teachers at what one might describe as the more traditional schools — with fewer ostensible "problems" and fewer concerns regarding pupils' participation.

The Sporting Ideology

As previously indicated, the vast majority of teachers in this study identified enjoyment as a central plank of their "philosophies". In addition, many saw enjoyment as crucial to young people's adherence to active lifestyles, and this was another key element in the teachers' ostensible "philosophies". It was noticeable at the same time, however, that for many it was simply taken for granted that the *enjoyment* would be of *sport*:

> Above all...for them to enjoy PE through a medium of participation in sports.

> They [the pupils] have to understand that...sport is to be enjoyed ...sport is enjoyable and something that is good.

Such views were typical of the amalgam of what I am referring to as justificatory ideologies which frequently incorporated unrecognised and irreconciled tensions; for example, an emphasis upon competitive team sport often sat somewhat uneasily alongside an avowed commitment to "enjoyment" and, at the same time, to "sport for all".

Even where participation was the primary concern of teachers, this tended to be participation in (competitive) *sport* and, frequently, team games. Indeed, physical activity and sport were regularly treated as synonymous:

> PE should be about getting children involved in physical activity and teaching them about different physical activities...[because] *that's what sport's all about isn't it?...children need to be taught sport and if they are not taught it in schools where are they necessarily going to learn about it? And it's getting them involved in sport and making them see that sport is...enjoyable* and it is accessible to them...because we are not going to have a fit and healthy nation [otherwise]...so that they will play in later life when they leave school...*I suppose what we are teaching them is about different sports* [emphases added].

By the same token, even where teachers possessed a strong commitment to widening access and to encouraging active lifestyles in the promotion of health, it is worthy of note that they frequently also had a strong commitment to sport and sports performance including the associated ideological leanings towards the alleged benefits of sporting competition:

> For as many people as possible...it's our job to educate the pupils [so] that when they leave school they [will] want to partake in *sport...to get all pupils to as high a level of performance as they can*...so everyone gets a chance...a "sport for all" philosophy [emphasis added].

On the whole, PE teachers' "philosophies" were nothing if not complex, even somewhat contradictory. As often appears to be the case with Government and Sports Council (now Sport England) policies in relation to young people and sport in schools, ideologies were often intertwined in an awkward and not altogether coherent framework. Various PE teachers (especially male) appeared to assume that competition was an important, almost essential, element of sport and, thus, PE. The importance of achieving competitive sporting success frequently appeared to dominate a number of teachers' thinking:

> I think it's brilliant having competitive sport in school; it's a real focus and it's a real drive for the children.

> We have been very successful over the years...if I don't get a team in the local finals I'll be *very, very* upset [emphasis in the original].

> And we are not going to drop netball because we are one of the most successful teams in [the county].

This was the case despite the fact that their responses often included claims to the contrary:

> I don't care about winning. I've never bothered about winning. *If you're doing your job then you win!*...I've got no time for elitism ...schools that we compete with they will often say that we're elitist because we tend to win everything [emphasis added].

Whilst, at first glance, some teachers' tendency to emphasise winning and success appeared to conflict with other aspects of their "philosophies", it did seem to reflect (a) the teachers' deep-seated convictions and values, (b) their perceptions regarding the traditions of PE, and (c) their perceptions of school expectations of PE.

The Tension between Performance and Participation

Given the complex, not to say confused, nature of teachers' "philosophies", it was unsurprising that tension between the potentially conflicting emphases upon performance and participation was an implicit theme running through many teachers' views. This tension became especially transparent in relation to extra-curricular PE[4], as I shall indicate later. Two quotations — from female and male teachers respectively — provide a flavour of this tension:

> Number one, we want *everyone to be involved in sport*; number two, *I don't like the idea of recreation*. I believe that the country is turning into armchair athletes and armchair footballers rather than actually going out and doing it...don't go away with the idea that it's the teams that worry me; that's just an extension, that's just the last one-tenth of it [emphases added].

> "Sport for all"...as many people involved as possible, *rather than just sort of getting teams out*...we want *excellence* but we want it across the board [emphases added].

One particular exchange provided a neat illustration of the confusing, even contradictory, ideas prevalent in some teachers' thinking, particularly that of males. Such views appeared to reflect an amalgam of an intuitive commitment to a notion of PE as *essentially* sport that had, nonetheless, been more-or-less penetrated by an amalgam of "sport for all", "education for leisure" and health

---

[4] Extra-curricular PE — or sport and physical activities done out of school hours (Sport England, 2001) — is probably most adequately defined as: "the provision of activities outside of the formal PE curriculum, most often after-school and at lunch-times, but also in some schools, at weekend and/or before school [by PE teachers]" (Penney and Harris, 1997, p. 42).

ideologies. An established male PE teacher offered the view that the emphasis on performance and skill acquisition in PE lessons was diminishing and added, "that's what we need to get back to …because the standard in those major team games is slipping". When I suggested to him that some of the teachers he was criticising (for allegedly moving away from "traditional" PE) would also claim that they were trying to encourage "sport for all" but through broader, more "recreational", "activity choice" approaches, he replied, "…so, what is the success rate of that attitude of getting pupils to actually *perform at any level* whatsoever?" (emphasis added). He continued:

> I mean, OK, you can go to the gym—that's fine for "fitness for life"…that's important but other things, like badminton…to get to any sort of standard you've got to actually give them the chance to go to clubs; a chance to be part of a team. Because that is what will happen in life: they will go to a club…will be involved with a team…but I don't see that after 3.20 pm — they go home; it doesn't happen!

This kind of view was expressed more directly by this teacher's HoD:

> What horrifies me is the general standard of PE in this country… I would say it's awful…year in year out, the same schools go to the finals. Now, every school does athletics, supposedly; every school does cricket, supposedly; every school is doing all of the sports and yet most schools don't achieve anything with their teams! Now, how can that be?

Of particular note was the manner in which such views involved very *particular* and *subjective*, that is to say, preferred, conceptions of what PE should be about; in this case and, once again, particularly with males, it was evidently sport and especially team games.

Acquisition of Sports Skills

The prevalence of a sporting ideology was reflected in some teachers' (both male and female but especially the former) emphasis upon the acquisition of skills in PE lessons. It was at this point that prior emphasis upon what might be described as the non-educational goals of enjoyment and sports performance began to incorporate more ostensibly educational goals. Many teachers in the study perceived the acquisition of sporting skills as being a central function of PE, particularly in the initial stage of secondary education (at Key Stage 3):

> From Year 7 to Years 8 and 9...they are increasing their repertoire of skills.

> ...learning basic skills. And if they don't get basic skills — the co-ordination — they are never going to get them. It's something we have to do. It's on the curriculum.

In similar vein, some teachers in Mason's (1995) study offered views contrasting with the educational orientation of others. Mason commented:

> some teachers held a more "skills training" view of PE, consistent with teaching pupils the basic skills of PE mentioned in the earlier stages of the National Curriculum. (Mason, 1995, p. 3)

Indeed, for some teachers in my study, skill acquisition remained the role of PE throughout their secondary-school life. Some made no attempt to hide their unequivocal commitment to the acquisition of sports skills in the face of recent developments (such as NCPE):

> Call me old school if you like but it's about *physical* education; it's about the *physical* and...[as] the old school say, "put the physical back into physical education" ... When I hear "plan, perform, evaluate", I'd go along with that to a degree, I mean they can plan things like in...gymnastics, but I don't think they can plan particularly well the movements for a [rugby] line-out...[performance] that's where I'm coming from [emphasis in the original].

It was interesting to reflect that this male teacher articulated a view implicit in a number of (particularly male) teachers' comments. Yet, at no time did a teacher intimate the contrasting view that might be summarised as "putting the *education* back into physical education". The clear impression one formed was that for many PE teachers the emphasis in PE is and should remain on the *physical* rather than the *educational*.

As was the case with a number of (typically male) PE teachers, in the eyes of the above teacher PE was "definitely" about skill acquisition. In this regard, it was interesting to note one teacher imply that learning was necessarily related to skill acquisition — anything else was not learning as such! This kind of view stands diametrically opposed to the academic definition of knowledge favoured by the views of those philosophers of education (and PE) whose line of thinking has come to represent the "standard" conception of education and in recent years, according to Reid (1996a, 1996b, 1997), the "new orthodoxy" in PE.

Skill acquisition remained close to the centre of a number of (yet again, particularly male) teachers' view of PE. As one teacher put it, sometimes lessons are about enjoyment and sometimes "it's much more serious":

> Sometimes I would explain to the kids that certain sessions…[are] about *learning*; this is *pure* physical education you know — *learning about how to do something* [emphases added].

Notwithstanding claims for the increased prevalence of the "teaching games for understanding" (TGFU) (otherwise known as games-sense games teaching) approach — notably among academics and teacher-trainers — it is clear that the conventional approach to pedagogy retains many loyal supporters, particularly among established male PE teachers:

> We warm up…we do certain skills that we are going to look at [in] that particular lesson and, then, if they behave, and all has gone well, we can finish [with a game] and they can take those skills that we've practised through to the game…and that will go through every games lesson.

> I'm the old school that says, "Right, warm them up, this is how you perform in a line-out, now go away and perform it"… They need to know certain moves for rugby, for soccer, for cricket, and I believe they should be taught rather than go away and plan them and then perform them.

Needless to say, many male PE teachers were "quite happy" with the renewed emphasis upon games in both the revised NCPE of 1995 and *Sport: Raising the game* (DNH, 1995).

Coaches, Coaching and the Sporting Ideology

The tension evident in teachers' comments related to the participation/performance emphasis was illustrated in their mixed views on the involvement of coaches in PE — a trend already in place before the publication of the Conservative Government's policy statement *Sport: Raising the game*, but further encouraged by that report as well as successive Governments' renewed emphasis upon "traditional" sport and team games in the curriculum (DNH, 1995; DCMS, 2000). It is noteworthy, however, that, on the whole, PE teachers appeared remarkably receptive to coaches being involved in PE. This is contrary to what one might expect, given that it implies that there is no a priori need for a specialist qualification in order to be involved in teaching PE and that this, in turn, might be seen as undermining teachers' claims for the kind of specialist professional status which has been something of a preoccupation with PE teachers over the years.

There are a number of practical reasons for this willingness to use coaches. Several teachers noted the growing links with coaches and the governing bodies of sport:

> We get a lot of offers, you know, "Can we come and do this, can we come in and do that?"

> There have been a lot of government schemes trying to encourage "sport for all"...*Raising the Game*...we have done lots of things like that. We've had all sorts of people coming in to school to give people basketball — Manchester Giants come, Chester Jets come — ... rugby league, we have cricket, dance people coming in ...

As with a number of other links between schools and their communities, the impetus for many of these developments, as reported by several teachers, came not so much from the academic or professional press but rather the "lots of flyers sent around the schools which has made a bigger influence" and the contacts made with schools by local coaches and clubs themselves.

Some teachers seemed equivocal about the inclusion of coaches. However, their perceptions appeared more likely to be influenced by some kind of cost–benefit analysis, rather than objections born of a philosophical distinction between teaching and coaching. It was interesting to note, then, that whilst expressing practical concerns, many teachers did not appear as threatened as one might have expected, nor, for that matter, to object in principle to the prospect of sports coaches becoming involved in PE:

> Teacher: Some [coaches] are good and some are bad, some have got a lot of knowledge but can't pass it over to the kids...some are absolutely brilliant and the kids get an awful lot from it, but you have to vet them, you really do. And I have to go to [coaches] sometimes and say, "I'm sorry, but I want you to do this rather than you just go out and show off your skills".
> KG: How do you feel about coaches coming into PE?
> Teacher: Some of them are excellent in their subject knowledge but

> when it comes to actually teaching it's a little bit different…I can't see them taking over, it's just a very good addition [to PE].

Several of the teachers who commented upon the issue of coach involvement appeared to take a view not dissimilar to that on "activity choice" in PE. One teacher indicated that it seemed more appropriate to have coaches coming in at Key Stage 4 and/or extra-curricular PE. Nonetheless, many teachers were quite happy for coaches to be involved at all levels of PE. Some teachers expressed the view that they would like to see coaches in because it was seen as helping maintain pupils' interest and motivation:

> If somebody [comes] in with new ideas – the whole place is buzzing!

> Teacher: I would love, absolutely love, more coaches to come in after school and help me.
> KG: What about in the curriculum?
> Teacher: I would love it.

Teachers expressing these kinds of views did not respond by outlining a *philosophical* justification for the involvement of coaches in the domain of teachers. Indeed, the justification was *no* justification as such. Rather, it was merely an outline of the *practical* benefits to the teacher of the involvement of coaches: that is to say, involving coaches in PE let some teachers "off the hook" – in terms of saving them work and/or providing "cover" for areas of inexpertise as well as helping with class motivation and control. In this regard, it was noteworthy that aspects of the justifications for the inclusion of coaches were similar to justifications for enjoyment as an aim inasmuch as the primary concerns of teachers appeared to be *pragmatic*.

Interestingly, those teachers most confident about the involvement of coaches were usually coaches themselves. They were, or had been, actively involved in coaching beyond the school setting and, on occasions, appeared to perceive themselves as coaches as much as teachers. In this regard, a number of the teachers appeared ready to turn a good deal of their teaching over to coaches – an attitude that would seem at once to undermine their claims to possess special skills. Several teachers' comments implied that they thought the quality of coaches had improved and that "these days" the quality of coaches was "far higher" because coaching courses had brought about an improvement in coaches' teaching skills. One teacher, unhappy with the pressures on her to perform onerous extra duties (additional to teaching and the extra-curricular work required when pupils are successful in county teams, for example), compared the situation in the UK unfavourably with the impression she had formed of PE in the USA, as delivered by teacher-coaches:

> [I was] much more impressed by it. It seems so much more professional and structured than it is here...they...have external people coming in to support them...they did a similar type of thing during the day but it appeared...that they only opted into the extra-curricular if they wanted to. So, they opted into running a school basketball team if they wanted. And it's fairly contractual — a contract would be signed...and they would be obliged to run...matches and...for that they would receive a payment...and you could opt out completely if you wanted to and just actually be the PE teacher and then they get external agencies in...like they do at some private schools here.

Bearing in mind what I have already suggested regarding PE teachers seeking practical solutions to practical problems, it is worth noting that adoption of such a system in the UK would, in effect, offer teachers the opportunity to opt out of the things they did not want to teach.

For some teachers in this study, distinguishing between the role of teacher and coach proved difficult. Indeed, one suspects that if some teachers had been able to find gainful employment in sports coaching, along the lines of the American education system, they would have pursued such a career path in preference to teaching:

> I would love to do that. I would love to be a coach who went into schools and taught trampolining...the overall standards would go up.

Describing himself as a coach as well as a teacher, and one who ran his own sports coaching business, one teacher commented that, "if the honest thing was said, I'd rather do that than teach". Implicitly revealing his own sporting ideology, he argued that PE specialists should be involved with children from the beginning of primary school, which, he claimed, would not only affect "sport for all" beneficially but would also "affect how many children are able to get to that sort of excellence stage if they want to". In this vein — and in line with government claims (DNH, 1995) regarding the alleged sporting orientation of PE teachers — he commented upon the benefits "of coaching from a qualified coach from an early age", and added, "until we do that sport won't progress in this country".

Invited to offer his views on coaches becoming involved in teaching, he responded:

> I'm biased on the point because I am a coach as well as a PE teacher. I feel that it would benefit schools and we've had instances of it here quite recently when we did cricket. A gentleman from the [local] cricket club offered to do sessions…three of the kids are suddenly part of [their] junior team.

He continued by making reference to what he saw as the role of coaches in developing talented children in areas where teachers do not have the requisite specialism:

> I certainly would not be able to take a good team and progress them further because I don't feel my personal ability, coaching-wise or cricket-wise, would allow me to do that. Whereas, if somebody comes in who's a good cricket coach…he's got the ability to take them further.

With regard to the teacher–coach issue, Penney and Harris (1997, p. 49) observe that:

> the long talked about divide between schools and clubs and between teachers and coaches in England and Wales has yet to be overcome. Lawson…identified…the "school perspective" as being "…the entitlement of *every school pupil* to be given the opportunity to develop skills to a level commensurate with his/her ability and inclination" and the "*NGB perspective*" as the creation of links that will assist towards a *talent identification programme* [emphases in the original].

My research, it must be said, did not entirely bear out such a conclusion. Teachers in this study subscribed to a range of views that could be taken, it is argued, to represent, more-or-less, several ideological clusters of meaning. At one end of the spectrum these were in line with those alluded to in Mason's (1995) report — where teaching and coaching were seen as quite distinct entities — and, at the other end, were those teachers who appeared to treat them as synonymous, and occasionally saw the latter as the essence of the former — as was the case with a good number of teachers in this study. At the same time, a number of teachers seemed to view "sport for all" as sitting quite easily alongside talent identification.

One area in which sporting ideologies were particularly in evidence was in teachers' views regarding extra-curricular PE, and it is to this that I now want to devote particular attention.

The Sporting Ideology and Extra-Curricular PE

Research (Mason, 1995; Penney and Harris, 1997; Roberts, 1996a; SCW, 1995) suggests that, in terms of the involvement of teachers and pupils alike, extra-curricular PE is alive and well. All of the teachers in my own study claimed to be heavily involved in extra-curricular PE. Indeed, many expressed the view that their professional (and, frequently, personal) lives were "dominated", almost blighted, by it. Despite this, it was interesting to note that a number of them (typically male) maintained the common-sense view of Government and media (see, for example, DNH, 1995; Carvel, 1999; Davies, 1999) that there had, indeed, been a degradation of extra-curricular PE since the so-called "teachers' dispute" of the mid-1980s:

> I think a lot of people packed up and didn't go back to extra-curricular. I mean some areas are now getting back to what they were but others are still well behind.

> But I know that outside it's getting more difficult to get...matches and extra-curricular things, because teachers aren't prepared to give up their time after school or at weekends or take part in matches.

Such a view was more apparent among teachers at schools with a strong sports orientation and commitment to competitive sports fixtures:

> KG: Are you convinced then that some teachers are not by and large doing extra-curricular?
> Teacher: They're not; they are definitely not. I mean you can look at football...to actually get fixtures...you're wasting your time.

There was a tendency among a number of teachers — especially those whose extra-curricula provision was particularly successful — to caricature provision (and, for that matter, the attitudes of teachers) at other schools:

> I'm sure not every PE teacher does it. I'm sure they say "Well, we're not going to enter X, Y and Z because we want to be home at 5.30pm with our feet up with our children". I'm sure a lot of people do. It's our own fault.

> Surely somewhere there's extra-curricular going on but I have not even met 40% of the teachers in the area because you never see them.

It was noteworthy that the perceptions of the above teachers contrasted markedly with the views of the teachers being carica-tured. Indeed, the caricature could only be said to apply to a very small number of teachers in the study; what Scotson and Elias (1994) might refer to as "the worst of the worst".

But what of PE teachers' "philosophies" regarding extra-curricular PE? It was noticeable that the broad consensus among PE teachers was that extra-curricular PE represented an *extension* of curricular PE. The view of extra-curricular PE as a continuation of curricular PE has, in my personal experience of teaching, long been commonplace among PE teachers and it continues to be so ("that's part of the job"). Almost without exception, PE teachers described extra-curricular PE thus:

> Well, it's extensions. [In] curricular PE we start off with the basics [skills] and develop it as we go through.

> To have any sort of extension you need to be partaking in extra-curricular — which is part of the job.

This view of extra-curricular activities as an extension of the curriculum programme is one shared and implicitly endorsed by OFSTED (1998). This much, then, was self-evident: for many PE teachers, extra-curricular PE was an "extension...of what we do". However, quite what the focus or foci of extra-curricular work should be was a little more difficult to establish. To put it another way, it was when one came to explore PE teachers' "philosophies" vis-à-vis the prac-tice of extra-curricular PE proffered that the picture became more opaque. The "philosophies" of PE teachers with regard to extra-curricular work were quite complex, not to say confused. Frequently, the views of teachers in the study reflected the supposedly multiple foci of extra-curricular work:

> It's another time when you can go and do some sports and exercise to extend what they're doing in [the curriculum], and give them an opportunity to participate against other schools.

> What we should be aiming to do here is to have it [extra-curricular] as an extension...just for participation...[but also] to actually set higher targets...skill-wise.

The final quotation illustrates the Janus-headed nature of extra-curricular PE. By "extension" PE teachers appeared to mean at least two things: extension in terms of a *continuation* and/or, more usu-ally, development "to a higher level" of (sports) *performance*:

> We offer an extended version of what we offer in lessons…we have netball teams, hockey teams, tennis teams.

> They [the pupils] are willing, they want to learn, so we do skills which you wouldn't normally do in the lesson time.

Whilst "continuity" was the ostensible rationale, the manner in which the principle of continuity manifested itself tells us something about the underpinning ideologies at work among teachers as well as the constraints surrounding practice. It was common, for example, for teachers who claimed continuity to stress nevertheless the desirability of a performance emphasis in extra-curricular work:

> Extra-curricular is more about elitism…[it should be about] competing against other schools… Having said that, to rounders club I'll get children who are keen… Well, ideally, it should be about a broad base again shouldn't it? Yes, well, when I think about it, yes: it should be about helping those children in different areas improve on skill and…push them a little bit further to compete.

Consistent with the findings of Penney and Harris (1997), the practice of PE teachers in my own study (if not always the "philosophies") revolved to a greater extent around sport, particularly team sports, and to a lesser extent around team practices. Nevertheless, a noticeable feature of the teachers' views was that, again almost without exception, they described extra-curricular PE as "open" to *all* pupils inasmuch as, ostensibly, any youngster could attend if they so desired. In this vein, teachers characteristically claimed a commitment to both "sport for all" *and* performance sport:

> There are practices every break-time, every lunch-time and virtually every night and at weekends. But it's not just for the teams, it's open — the whole school can take part.

> Extra-curricular activities…are skill-based, selective…but [we] also have open practices as well. So, if someone feels they wouldn't get into a team or they are not very good, they can still come to these practices. [They're] not just for so-called team players…it's…open practices. So, the pupils, whatever level, can turn up to do something.

In claiming this dual commitment, many teachers not only stressed the *equal weighting* given to both "sport for all" and performance sport but felt able to reconcile the two:

> I think that…you should have…the school teams etc. but there's got to

> be the recreational side — like a badminton club on one night — anybody can come along, anybody can take part, there's no competition to it.

Indeed, a good number of teachers argued that one led to the other:

> But your teams come out of the open clubs. All the clubs here are open, any pupils can come.

> [Extra-curricular PE is]*very, very* important; and for a large number of children to be involved. Extra-curricular is *really, really* important...we really struggle, to get team practices in... The school is a very small school but a large number...of staff are involved in extra-curricular, especially the PE side. And, because this is happening, clubs take just as much importance as teams — loads of clubs. And also we're encouraging as many people to come to practices as possible...anyone can come, it's not a team practice, anyone can come... Our teams could be stronger if we didn't allow...as many as possible [to come]. And we fill a coach. So that it's not year 7 "A" team netball going off — we've got A, B, C and D teams going [emphases in the original].

Similar to the manner in which PE teachers appeared quite ready to embrace the use of coaches in PE, they were also keen to develop links with sports clubs:

> Connections with outside clubs...is something we try and steer people towards.

Among the teachers there were some unequivocal expressions of commitment to what might be termed "sport for all" (along the lines of the Sports Council's strategy of recent decades with which it was associated):

> I just want to get as many people as involved as possible. I'm not bothered whether they are brilliant teams or whatever, I just want to try and get everybody to like PE.

However, these were relatively rare. Indeed, even here, whilst the philosophy was one of "sport for all", the putative practice centred upon sport and competitive team games. It became clear that, notwithstanding professed commitment to involving as many pupils as possible in extra-curricular activity, there was a tension here that had, unsurprisingly, not been thought through, for nothing constrained teachers to reconcile the apparently irreconcilable. Extra-curricular PE provided teachers with a degree of freedom to choose and they chose sport. This predisposition was, in turn, exacerbated by constraints in the form of the expectations and requirements of various groups, prominent amongst which were head teachers and parents.

Despite outward expressions of commitment to "open" practices and "sport for all", an emphasis on *performance* was clearly evident in teachers' "philosophies" as well as in their professional practices:

> The importance is on *performance* and getting people to get involved in sport [emphasis added].

> The ones that are more able can come to the extra-curricular activities and I can push them on...beyond the Key Stage.

And this was not merely an emphasis upon performance. It tended also to be an emphasis upon performance in *competitive* sports and particularly *team* games:

> We do most clubs, apart from athletics. We do a lot of netball.

However, whilst "clubs" can refer to, "badminton clubs, gym clubs, dance clubs", in practice it usually meant team games and team practices:

> We run so many teams as it is, we don't have the time to meet all the sports...so we...point them in the direction of clubs.

> [Extra-curricular is] *very, very* weighted towards team games [emphasis in the original].

> A lot of it's teams...but we do try to keep clubs going for such activities as trampolining...very, very popular...[but] I find my time is taken with team games.

Penney and Harris (1997, p. 43) claim that extra-curricular PE, "is dominated by traditional team games, invariably has a competitive focus and is also 'gendered'". Accordingly, they argue that this "particular focus" results in extra-curricular PE "*offering limited opportunities to only a minority of pupils*" (Penney and Harris, 1997, p. 43; emphasis in the original) — a minority of students who tend, as it were, to select themselves.

Even when teachers acknowledged that their extra-curricular provision favoured team practices and inter-school matches, they appeared keen to add a caveat regarding "sport for all": "But even at team practices anybody is welcome. It's not just the team that come." It is illuminating to note, however, that this teacher acknowledged that in practice:

> it does end up like that, they [the elite girls] are the team…and the others are not welcome. So, although we have team practices we still hope those people will come but they don't. But then we've got more of a weighting towards the team but they are still opportunities for people just to come along [to] non-team clubs.

> [Extra-curricular PE is] recreational based. We will have football practice from which we will select a team…[but] anybody who wants to come along may do so; *although, in reality, it is nearly always the team* [emphasis added].

Teachers also seemed aware that the participant profile of pupils attending extra-curricular PE (that is to say, the more able) acts as one more barrier to the less able:

> The ones that stand out are the ones that come to extra-curricular. They are the ones that create teams and I just think that situation puts a lot of people off.

The profile of participants appeared to serve as some kind of self-fulfilling prophecy that reinforced the sporting ideology of many teachers.

All in all, it was apparent that despite teachers' rhetoric — regarding the ostensible "sport for all" orientation of extra-curricular PE — practice was clearly biased towards *sport*, especially team games, rather than *exercise*, and was *competitive sport* rather than *recreation* oriented in nature. Penney and Harris conclude that:

> …the focus of extra-curricular provision is competition between single sex teams representing different schools. Furthermore…this focus is also competition in "traditional", "gendered" and primarily "invasion" games… It is games such as rugby, football, netball and hockey that dominate. (1997, p. 46)

Penney and Harris's description of extra-curricular PE is supported by the findings here and elsewhere (see, for example, Mason, 1995; Sport England, 2001).

In part, this apparent bias can be explained in terms of inheritance, the continuation of tradition. It is also, however, a reflection of the pre-eminence of a sporting ideology in teachers' "philosophies", in figuration with the various constraints they experience at the local and national levels.

One interview provided a particularly useful insight into the complex and multi-faceted pressures on PE teachers in relation to "sport for all", active lifestyles and sports performance:

> I do feel that we go over the top. We allow the extra-curricular to, not exactly dominate, but it does take a fairly high profile in this school…we [the department] [decided]…a while back now…that all children should have the opportunity to do extra-curricular activity at least once a week and we've endeavoured to do that. And I think really, with hindsight, we are too small a department to carry that through.

But it is not simply a *tension* that is apparent; frequently *confusion* also appears close to the surface:

> Extra-curricular activity is for children who want to do [PE]; who want to be taken that much further. My lessons would obviously cater for them as much as I possibly could, but PE lessons are for everybody as far as I'm concerned, regardless of ability… [Extra-curricular] is the chance I get to spend [time] with the kids who want to [do PE]…the more *able* kids, all the kids who want to come along and have *fun* [emphases added].

Having spoken at length and with feeling about his concern that PE — especially at Key Stage 4 — should introduce youngsters to a range of activities that they might take with them into later life, one teacher outlined an extra-curricular programme that provided what he termed "opportunity". And yet, seemingly unaware of the potential tension between the two positions, he went on to comment:

> We are quite competitive. We play netball…football in the main. But we do cross-country, athletics, we have the occasional basketball… We do cricket, rounders, tennis, athletics — we run as much as we can… The majority are team-based, but we run practices that are open — anyone can come along, it's not just…the team players… There are clubs that are not team-based, like badminton club, table tennis club, gym club.

He added:

> I must admit *I still like competition*, even after having said all that. I think children thrive on competition — life is a competition, really. So, I like the competition… I'm still a competitive person myself. I was brought up that way. But I understand that *there's people out there who are not that way inclined*; we offer the other clubs for them *when we can* [emphases added].

This view was not at all uncommon and the tension was implicit in the comments of a number of teachers; for example:

> The aerobics, the circuit-training, they're all pretty good fun, but we used to have competitions, aerobics competitions. We do rhythmic gymnastics — then we have a competition for that. So, we're doing it as a recreational thing really; at the end we have a competition to decide the best... It's netball practice on Thursday night and we have team practice...then I organise matches on a Tuesday night.

It is in extra-curricular PE, Penney and Harris (1997) suggest, where the "fundamental link" as they describe it, between PE and sport — often implicit, frequently explicit, in official and semi-official pronouncements — "is arguably most visible" (p. 42). Indeed, it is tempting to observe that in some cases it might be more adequate to describe extra-curricular PE not so much as a PE–sport link but, rather, as a sport–sport link. This is perhaps best illustrated by the comments of a teacher from a very successful school (in sporting terms): "I don't differentiate between lessons and extra-curricular, I just carry on". He added:

> The PE department here work right through the day. The break-time here is just another session. So, at the moment, I'll do high jump in the gym because I can have my coffee and as many kids as want can come in...the whole day is just an extension of what I do — that is, *coach sport* [emphasis added].

On occasions explicitly, but more often implicitly, it became clear that for a substantial number of teachers (usually, but by no means always, men) extra-curricular PE was not so much "the icing on the cake" as the primary concern of teachers. Or, rather, what they were "free" to do in extra-curricular PE — in essence, sport — was more like what *curricular* PE *should* consist of, as far as they were concerned:

> In some cases...extra-curriculum is sort of like the "head"...the curricular [PE] is not the main focus.

> If we do our jobs properly we should have people knocking at the door to do extra-curricular activities.

Penney and Harris echo the Sports Council for Wales's (SCW) concern that this tendency "exacerbates the previously existing imbalance as extra-curricular sport seems to be becoming ever more competitive and geared to performance" (SCW, 1995; cited in Penney and Harris, 1997, p. 44) and, consequently, is biased towards and favours the minority of pupils with particular sporting ability.

Whatever the merits or demerits of such a development, it seems indisputable that—as several commentators have pointed out (Mason, 1995; Penney and Harris, 1997; SCW, 1995)—extra-curricular PE *is* biased towards sport and, within sport, towards team games, not least because many PE teachers like it that way and are more constrained towards such practice than they are constrained away from it.

The Academic Ideology

To the extent that teachers offered academic justifications for PE in their "philosophies", these tended to take two broad forms: what might be termed personal and social education and examinations in PE or, as I will refer to it here, examinable PE.

The Academic Ideology and the "Silent Curriculum"

Where the academic ideology was discernible (even tangentially) in PE teachers' "philosophies", it typically took the conventional form (see Blake, 1996; Laker, 1996a, 1996b; Munrow, 1972) of faith among teachers in the utility (supposedly inherent in sport) for the development of the moral and social dimensions of youngsters' characters. Many of the claims for the alleged moral and character-development benefits of PE made by teachers bore the hallmarks of the kind of fantasy-laden thinking characteristic of ideology. Occasionally explicitly, but more frequently implicitly, teachers outlined their beliefs that mere involvement in PE—and especially sport and team games—would be sufficient to bring about what schools often label personal and social education (PSE).[5]

The belief, put colloquially, that PE reaches the parts that other subjects cannot, in terms of "building up the character", as one teacher put it, was quite commonplace. For many teachers this was seen as a kind of informal but nevertheless significant aspect of the PE curriculum:

> Teacher: It's like a silent curriculum, the social side of it—it's in our handbook...we do work at it but it's obviously not in the written curriculum.

---

[5] With Curriculum 2000, PSE became known as personal, social and *health* education (PSHE). This reflects governmental desire to incorporate health issues into PSE (see The Qualifications and Curriculum Authority [QCA], 1999).

> KG: What is in the written curriculum?
> Teacher: It's just skills, really...sports skills...The social skills are what
> you would call the "silent curriculum".

A variety of features of this supposed process of socialisation were identified, such as the benefits of co-operation for pupils' sociability:

> Working as a team... Co-operation through relationship building... I
> think that on the way, actually taking part in these things, you gain a
> lot more...than "I just play netball, I just play football"... It's
> something for life that you are trying to promote, not just for now...
> the skills that you achieve will help you in other areas of life as well.

Thus, involvement in PE and sport was taken by teachers to propagate "a lot of social skills" as well as "an opportunity to develop their all-round character":

> I think that people should be able to participate [for] all sorts of
> reasons...the health reason to start off with...that's a fairly high profile
> at the moment isn't it? But also there is all the social skills and
> everything else...it's the whole person development.

Such a view was expressed particularly forcibly by teachers in the relatively disadvantaged schools in the study:

> In [this area] it's even more of a priority, because a lot of the kids are
> quite antisocial, so you put them in situations where they depend
> upon each other for their success.

> because a lot of them don't know how to mix socially, how to play with
> others, how to team up with others.

Some teachers in schools with a particular religious "mission" also emphasised the supposed PSE benefits of sport and PE:

> We talk about the school motto..."Do unto others as you would have
> done unto you" and we follow that motto in our teaching to the kids.

Sport (for it was usually sport rather than PE that was mentioned in this respect) was frequently claimed by teachers to be analogous with life ("[sport] can be associated with life, really"). The character-developing benefits of experiencing an allegedly "natural", all-pervasive (and by implication, beneficial) feature of social life — competition — in the form of a game, was also to the fore in teachers' comments:

> The competitive side of sport which...in other subjects...in school you
> don't necessarily get and obviously you get that when you leave

> school in your jobs…you're going to get benefit from…social, competitive challenge…which are all interlinked to participation in sport.

In addition, a sense of achievement was expected to flow from sporting success:

> A feeling of personal achievement, helping the social skills, the social interaction, helping their self-confidence, finding something they're good at.

Once again, this was particularly prominent amongst teachers faced with the perceived constraints of working in disadvantaged areas:

> giving them [pupils] a sense of achievement…for the lower [ability] end…teamwork and getting on with each other… It's a sense of achievement for them if they are good at sport but not so academically.

In this regard, teachers frequently suggested that PE might bring pupils "out of themselves", enabling "the quieter ones", "the more introverted pupils", to find something they're good at to "improve their self-awareness and self-esteem" and to take "leadership" roles. Several teachers commented upon the professed "knock-on" effects of success in sport for academic school work:

> If they're achieving through sport, through physical activity…then they can go on to achieve academically, they can achieve in terms of their future and they can set themselves goals and they can set themselves targets.

PE was perceived by the teachers as an ideal vehicle for encouraging young people to "develop themselves", on the basis that this was what they considered sport to have done for them throughout their lives:

> I went down the rugby road and rugby opened up so many avenues in terms of personal strengths, not only the physical side, which I believe is very important…it gave me a lot of confidence… I went…from strength to strength…and I believe that sport gives that to children…I believe sport is important from that point of view…they gain confidence, organisational skills. It opened up other avenues… friendships.

It was also noticeable, however, that many teachers who claimed PSE benefits for PE, when asked if they could identify it in their practice, answered, "Don't think so, no". Even those who claimed they could then tended to describe it as happening indirectly or unconsciously:

> KG: Can you recognise yourself doing moral development and aesthetic development in your lesson?
> Teacher: Yes, I think I would. Definitely, yes. I don't think you're conscious in saying, "Yes, I must get moral development". I think what happens is it [just] comes out of what's happened.

The way in which this teacher elaborated upon this point – by offering an example of a girl being "stumped on fourth base", being annoyed, throwing her rounders bat away and the lessons the pupil allegedly learned as a result, in this case about the need to try harder next time – was typical of the anecdotal evidence teachers tended to supply, almost as an afterthought.

What was particularly striking about what I am referring to as teachers' claims for the contribution of PE to PSE was the impression one formed of a somewhat idealised view of the process. In addition, the manner in which teachers' responses were often quite delayed – as if they were struggling to find practical examples – seemed to suggest more of an eclectic "clutching at straws" approach to justifying PE in PSE terms. Similarly striking was the impression that the rather vague responses to questions regarding the ability of the teachers to recognise examples of PSE in PE in *practice* suggested that external agencies such as OFSTED would be even less convinced of their efficacy. Academics (such as Laker, 1996a, 1996b), as well as a number of teachers, might continue to claim its existence in theory but it seems that many would have difficulty – as, indeed, teachers in this study did – finding examples from teachers' professed practice.

Whilst I have chosen to use the term PSE because of its currency in secondary schools as a formal process for bringing about the kinds of objectives PE teachers were claiming for PE, it is worth noting, nonetheless, that they themselves did not make this connection explicitly or otherwise. This is something one might reasonably have expected them to do had they really believed in the efficacy of PE in PSE terms. Rather, they appeared to turn to PSE more as an afterthought, seemingly utilised to bolster their preferred views with a more overtly educational rationale.

The Academic Ideology and Examinable PE
An added dimension to what I am calling the academic ideology

within teachers' "philosophies" was their concern with examinable PE. One of the more dramatic developments in secondary PE over the past 30 years has been the growth, one might even say explosion, of examinations, particularly at GCSE and A level (Carr, 1997; Green, 2001; Mackreth, 1998; Reid, 1996a). The last decade, in particular, has witnessed marked growth, both in terms of pupil examinees and exam centres.

The first point to note regarding the teachers' views on examinations in PE is that many were keen to claim the kind of educational justifications for the development of GCSE and A level PE and sports studies. Increasing opportunities for those pupils with ability in PE was offered as a common justification for examinable PE:

> Well…it's about choice, and pupils are given a choice and we want to offer them that extra choice.

> It gives…another window for someone who's interested in PE — who did PE to get some success…they can't get elsewhere.

A related justification was the alleged opportunity examinable PE provided for pupils to obtain a qualification in something that they were good at:

> We have children with a lot of talent and I think it's important that they should be able to manifest…[what] they have talent in.

In addition, examinable PE was claimed to have potential vocational benefits for pupils:

> They can get a qualification in it…[which] prepares them for the leisure industry and PE teaching.

Insofar as teachers' concern with examinable PE formed part of their "philosophies", it might be viewed as an aspect of the academic ideology identifiable in teacher's views of PE. It was noticeable, however, that such ostensibly educational justifications for examinable PE were, at the same time, frequently bound up with more pragmatic justifications related to the standing of PE:

> I knew that there [were] pupils here…that [would] excel in it and I knew we were going to get [good] exam results…and now we've introduced A level, and all the time it's having a positive effect on the PE department and it's giving pupils something they have not had before.

Notwithstanding their ostensible concern with "choice" and "opportunity", the overriding impression one formed in discussion with the teachers was the manner in which their thoughts tended to revolve around their individual and collective concerns with what might be viewed as two sides of the same coin: professional status and public standing. In responding to the question "Why do you do examinable PE?", many teachers volunteered responses that had a good deal more to do with the status of PE, both internally and externally, than with pupil choice or even abstract academic justifications:

> KG: Why did you bother with examinable PE?
> Teacher: I agree, why bother!
> KG: So why have you bothered?
> Teacher: Credibility of the department.
> KG: Has it worked?
> Teacher: Yes…we're quite fortunate that we've had three years of very good students.

> KG: Why are you doing examinable PE?
> Teacher: To increase the profile of PE within school…people are seeing us now not just as [sports] people…because now we can be classed properly as an academic subject. It does have a knock-on effect, especially when the results come through.

Examinable PE was perceived by teachers as having the potential to raise both their own status and that of their department and subject —"especially" if "involved with the A level". In this vein, several suggested that the more demanding the theoretical aspect of the work, the greater the status attached — both in the eyes of colleagues and significant others:

> I think it raises the profile of PE, not just [with] students but for other members of staff as well.

> Pupils can't believe how much theory and written work they have to do — it's a big shock to the system. So…it does give us credibility.

This was a common response — the greater the degree of academic difficulty contained therein, the greater the level of esteem attached to examinable PE:

> When they [colleagues] look at the paper at invigilation, they are astounded…some of the comments you get from the other staff are: "At least we're working with an intelligent PE department!"… "they're academic people, it's just that they've chosen to do a practically based subject".

Nonetheless, the perceived requirement to do what "needed" to be done, rather than what one might "ideally" do, was a common cause for concern among PE teachers in this study. The ostensibly reluctant acceptance of pragmatism over principle was evident in the air of resignation exemplified by the following response:

> It probably does…give you a sort of status [as] an academic subject, but it shouldn't have to…the status of it in school is very low down. You get the jibes about "all you do is play all day"…but I think a lot of PE teachers are quite academic in a lot of ways…probably one way of proving it is the fact that we take an academic subject [examinable PE] and get success in it. But, it's a shame it has to be that way. It's a shame people don't *see PE for it's worth* [emphasis added].

Thus, the views of teachers in my own study regarding examinable PE reflected concerns with status over and above the putative educational and personal benefits for pupils. In this respect, the teachers' acceptance of, and enthusiasm for, examinable PE was somewhat at odds with their overall views on what PE should be about (their "philosophies").

The Gender Dimension to PE Teachers' "Philosophies"

It is worthy of note that there was a clear gender dimension evident in teachers' "philosophies", particularly with regard to their perceptions and claims regarding what was taught in the name of PE. According to a female HoD, the boys' department at her school tended to do "football most of the time" whereas the girls' provision was seen as far broader. Several female teachers offered comments reinforcing the view that, in their eyes at least, girls received a broader range of sporting and activity experience than boys on the whole. Nonetheless, it was apparent that much of girls' PE remained quite traditional in practice:

> Netball, hockey. That's the two main winter sports [for girls]. We don't do any sort of football or anything like that, or basketball. We concentrate on netball, hockey, gymnastics and dance and cross-country obviously…[we] like to develop pupils in…the traditional female sport[s].

Female teachers (and, occasionally male teachers) were inclined to explain the alleged broader provision for girls in terms of commitment:

KG: What would you put it down to?
Teacher: Commitment...to PE and offering the best and offering them [girls] a broader opportunity.

Several (mostly younger) female teachers took the view that the male side of their departments needed "new" and younger teachers if provision for boys' PE was to be broadened beyond an emphasis upon sport and team games and, by implication, improved:

> I think it needs new staff... I think the boys especially miss out on a lot of things. The girls get a lot... I think it's a shame the boys don't get what they should get.

> [The department needs] young male role-models for the boys.

Both female and male teachers reported that the former were more prepared to teach dance and gym and thus "[girls] get more opportunity" to do dance and gymnastics. Dance and gymnastics appeared to be the only areas that were frequently taught in mixed-sex groupings. Although several teachers reported that their departments "mixed up [*sic*] the boys and the girls", this, it was alleged, tended to be for dance and gymnastics and a selection of other activities:

> The girls did hockey and the boys did rugby. But they did dance...they had mixed dance. They did gymnastics together, they did basketball together — because they had done it from Year 7.

It is worthy of note that there appeared to be fewer equal opportunities outside the formal PE curriculum: that is to say that, perhaps unsurprisingly, more gender differentiation seemed (on the basis of teachers' claims) present in extra-curricular *sport* than in National Curriculum *physical education*:

> Pretty much [all extra-curricular clubs are] single sex and that's our [male] Head of Department's choice.

> [Boys] get football and they get basketball...the girls get dance, hockey, netball and football...I do think that the girls get[ting] a lot causes a bit of a "stir", [especially] getting the football thing together!

Whilst many female, as well as male, PE teachers appeared to prefer single-sex lessons, a number of female teachers commented upon the supposed lack of opportunity for girls to get involved in activities beyond the traditional girls' curriculum:

> There's definitely an attitude in this school…[it's for] the boys and it's not for the girls… It's OK for the girls to go and watch the boys play football but it's not alright for the girls to play football themselves. It's definitely that kind of mentality. And I think that's the area…and I think that's where we lose out a little bit.

Nonetheless, several teachers reported that they were offering football to girls and it was seen as being very popular:

> I did give them a couple of weeks where I gave them a choice…and they all wanted to [do football].

> Girls have had a lot of success in soccer, so I don't feel that I should stop them having that success just because it's not a traditional girls' game.

At one established female HoD's school, girls could "do some football" and the intention was to offer them cricket at some stage in the future:

> Equal opportunities…that's the way things are going now – a lot more girls teams. For the first time this year they are setting up a Cheshire League and a Halton League for girls. So, in order that our girls can progress to that…lower down [the school]…[we will do] the skills so that later on they can play that.

Several teachers claimed that offering girls a choice of less traditional activities often resulted in greater participation, and not simply in gender stereotypical activities. One teacher described how, at her school, girls could choose aerobics and multi-gym and that "quite a lot of them" chose multi-gym. Female teachers also alleged that this frequently created tension with male colleagues especially. In this regard it was apparent that the comment proffered by a male HoD represented only a slight caricature of the perspectives of a number of established male teachers:

> We despair when we see boys playing football with girls at some schools…because, quite clearly, the girls can't cope with the boys physical presence and the boys are not working the way they should be because girls are present. And they say, "It's because we haven't got enough PE teachers", and "This is the way the head wants us to teach", and "It's because we've got this equality clause in our school". Well, that's theorized on absolute nonsense… I've got a girl here who plays for England but I wouldn't coach her in lessons. I will not have girls doing football here because we will go down the mediocrity path. She

> will do the traditional girls' lessons: netball, hockey, dance, gymnastics and so on. Now she can then come out and do football at lunchtime if I've got someone to coach her in a girls situation. It does not matter about equal opportunities—I'm not interested. And people come and say that it's not an "equal opportunities" school and I say, "So what?"

Thus, it was readily apparent that various female teachers perceived male teachers as not as interested in PE (for example, gymnastics and dance) anything like as much as sport and games and that some male teachers concurred with this impression. This perception was implicitly endorsed by several male HoDs who commented on the difficulty they would face trying to get the "older" men to change their ways in line with the requirements of NCPE in relation to dance and Outdoor and Adventurous Activities (O&AA), for example. Whilst stressing that "not all men" she had taught alongside held such stereotypical orientations towards boys' and girls' PE, one well-established female teacher added that it was, nevertheless, typical of a large percentage of the many she had worked with over the course of her career. Indeed, this teacher was by no means alone in commenting that male teachers, when it came to outside "inspections" of their work, might "talk a good game" (as another teacher put it) but their practice was markedly different:

> They [male teachers] could say one thing…because they felt they ought to say it to you but…what they deliver in a lesson! I do think in a lesson the majority of the time they would just go out and "knock hell" with the boys and they couldn't give a "toss" about the National Curriculum… Generally, most bloke PE teachers are just…quite happy to go out with the lads and have a game of rugby and have a game of football.

In this regard, another teacher commented that her impression of the gap that she perceived, on the part of male PE teachers, between rhetoric and reality had been reinforced by the example of her brother, who she said was now lecturing at a college. She concluded:

> Well, we're just different, women and men are different and the way we approach jobs are different… The blokes are still happy to go out…a bit of a run around…hacking the ball about on the football pitch. They do keep some skills because they have got to be seen to be doing it but they will…not be so concerned about the content of their lesson.

For many teachers the differences were not just in *what* they claimed to teach but also the *way* they claimed to teach. An exchange with one teacher neatly illustrated many female teachers' perceptions of the gender differences in *modus operandi*:

> KG: [Do] you think that the view you have [the "philosophy"] is shared within the department [at] this school?
> Teacher: By the three women staff — yes, definitely.
> KG: And by the men?
> Teacher: No, I don't think so... With [the] boys [the male teachers] will say: "Oh, let's go and play a game". Whereas, I think, with female teachers they'll say, "No. We need to learn more about it rather than just playing a game."

It was interesting to note that a male teacher appeared to view the varied teaching styles employed by female PE teachers as a pragmatic response to the constraints of teaching girls' PE:

> I think on the female side they have had problems with getting girls to do PE. So, therefore, they have got to be more variable in their approach to lessons; they can't just get away with saying like, "Today we are going to do this" and talk for about five minutes about the skill because the girls haven't got the listening capabilities. So, I think the female members of staff have been a lot more diverse in their approach to lessons, which I think makes it more enjoyable for pupils.

Various female PE teachers claimed, by contrast, that female teachers in general were more concerned with the principles said to lie behind movement rather than actually performing and improving skills:

> In girls' PE it's more to do with understanding why you are doing it, how you are going to reach that final end of doing a cartwheel or whatever... I'm not saying it doesn't go on [in boys' PE] but they go through the stages and it's not explained as a principle of why you are doing it, rather than "you do this, you do that".

In this regard, it was interesting to note the perceptions of both male and female teachers (but especially the latter) that male teachers have not embraced other aspects of NCPE (or "best practice" for that matter), such as "performance, planning and evaluation", to the same extent as female teachers:

> I'm not at odds with the ladies department in this school, but they want to plan, perform and evaluate and I want to teach rugby, soccer.

I'm a bit of a games man and I *am* the acquisition of skills; *perform*, and *then* evaluate if necessary [emphasis in the original].

An exchange with one female teacher illustrated comments that were more commonplace than one might have anticipated – among both female and male teachers – with regard to the inherent capabilities and interests of boys and girls:

> They are so different, just innately different…because boys are so innately competitive – and I wouldn't have said that without having had the experience of it…they want to be competitive, whereas with the girls you are actually trying to get them to be competitive [which has]…to come secondary because you are trying to make them enjoy it first. But if you make it too competitive too early on that takes away their enjoyment and they will actually stop wanting to play. Now it's different with girls [in] teams because they are automatically the more competitive ones in the group… For the girls enjoyment and social interaction would be first, skill[s] would be next…and with the boys I think you are looking more at skill first…which would take them into later life, then interaction; because they are so competitive they help each other along.

With regard to the gender dimension of PE teachers' "philosophies", the data from this study support the claim that developments in academic theory in relation to gender "have had little impact on the prevailing ideas relating to gender differences in PE" among PE teachers (Waddington, Malcolm and Cobb, 1998, p. 34). Indeed, the "philosophies" and practices of many PE teachers continue to bear the hallmark of gender stereotyping in relation to their perceptions of male- and female-appropriate activities. In addition, significant differences were evident in the "characteristic pedagogical models" of male and female teachers in the study, similar to those reported by Evans, Davies and Penney (1996) and Waddington *et al.* (1998).

Conclusion

In this chapter I have attempted to identify and describe the everyday "philosophies" of PE teachers on the basis of data obtained from a study in the late 1990s. The first point to note is that, as expected, PE teachers rarely had anything that can be called a "philosophy" as such. Confusion and contradiction were common features of their views. What PE teachers articulated was typically a kind of checklist of aims, frequently centring upon words and phrases like "enjoyment", "health", "skills" and "character". If one were to be kind one might describe this as what Reid (1997) has referred to as "value pluralism" — a multiplicity of justifications for PE based on a plurality of values such as health, sports performance and character development. It seems more likely, however, that the teachers in this study did not possess the kinds of coherent, reflexive "philosophies" suggested by Reid's axiological outline. Rather, it seems that, in practice, PE teachers seized on convenient *ex post facto* rationalisations or justifications for the things they *did*! In this sense, it appeared that the "philosophy" followed the practice, rather than vice versa — as might conventionally be expected.

Many "philosophies" incorporated several ideas or ideologies. Frequently these "philosophies" emphasised one dimension, such as sport, among an amalgam featuring several additional aspects, such as health or PSE. The following examples illustrate the kinds of amalgam "philosophies" that were relatively commonplace. The initial examples are illustrative of a view that incorporates sport, health and "education for leisure" (in which sport is implicitly taken to incorporate health):

> ...providing children with positive habits throughout their life, positive sporting habits. That includes things like healthy eating, education on smoking, so not just strictly exercise; it has more wider-related issues... [The] number one aim as a teacher is to teach pupils various sporting skills and then...to enjoy it more, enjoy coming to the lessons...then probably the third would be to motivate them to do things.

> It should be giving pupils the best opportunity to take part in physical activity...for health...it's part of holistic growth of people. If they're not involved in PE they can't expect to be a person I don't think; if they're not physical as well as mental. The intellectual side of them can't be addressed just in classes. Intellectual growth is all about other things as well...it's just as important; in some ways, even more important.

Other amalgam "philosophies" incorporated an emphasis upon PSE in particular. An example was provided by the teacher who described personal development and health education as her two main aims, but who laid particular stress on PSE:

> I think it's an extremely good way for pupils to develop self-confidence in physical ability, in terms of relationship building, in

terms of learning to co-operate with others…a way of believing in themselves, having achievement and…recording that achievement… In terms of self-esteem it does them a lot of good. In terms of keeping themselves healthy for the future, I think it is extremely important.

Yet other amalgam "philosophies" took fitness as a substantial aspect of their focus:

KG: What do you think PE should be about?
Teacher: Teaching skills…keeping children fit and teaching social skills as well.
KG: Why?
Teacher: Well, we're all trying to maintain a reasonable fitness — that's part of life. We try to educate them to stay fit in all three areas, really: strength, stamina, suppleness. The social side: they have to work with each other in life, they play games and have to get on with each other — that's a strong philosophy of mine really… We work on that a lot in our department… I put social first, fitness second and skills third, really.

Many mixed "philosophies" — and particularly those of male teachers — emphasised sport and the development of sporting skills:

Well, first and foremost…I think enjoyment has got to be one of the key issues; acquisition of skills — obviously — and teamwork/co-operation. Obviously fitness is…mixed in with all that as well…to play sport, to carry out skills, you've got to have a certain amount of fitness.

The main thing I think people should get out of PE is enjoyment…in games situations and…within their own individual skills; whether that's in individual sport or games…[plus] being active learning skills…[so] they will do it outside of school.

The bottom line: I would like them to enjoy it, have some fun…increase their heart rate…and, thirdly…actually learn something as well…some skills or tactics or game-situations…[so that] they will carry on after they have finished at school.

The existence of continuities alongside (and somewhat despite) change appears a characteristic of ideological trends in the history of PE in the UK. Several distinguished commentators claim that real change occurred in the ideologies and practices of PE teachers in the last 15 to 20 years (Evans, 1992; Kirk, 1992a). It seems true to say that HRE, in particular, has assumed a more prominent place in the "philosophies" and practices of PE teachers. At the same time, "education for leisure" and "sport for all" (Hendry, Shucksmith, Love and Glendenning, 1993; Scraton, 1992), together with the promotion of active lifestyles, have become more central rationales for PE. Nevertheless, we can identify the persistence of widespread continuities alongside the occurrence of real change (see, for example, Curtner-Smith, 1995; Roberts, 1995, 1996a, 1996b; SCW, 1995). Sport, and especially team games, continues to be the most prominent activity area in the vast majority of curricula for boys and girls in secondary schools and lies at the heart of many teachers' "philosophies" of PE, albeit alongside other justificatory ideologies.

The best evidence regarding the extent of change — especially in PE teachers' "philosophies" but also in their practices — may well be provided by the way in which NCPE has been implemented at the level of the school as well as what happens in extra-curricular PE (Penney and Harris, 1997). And the evidence suggests the persistence of a sporting ideology. This should not be altogether surprising, for it is important to note that, whilst a comparison of the everyday "philosophies" of PE teachers with those of academic philosophers of PE might be seen to imply similar processes, this is far from the case.

Perhaps the most extensive and most recent study of PE teachers' "philosophies" is to be found in the Sports Council's *Young people and sport in England, 1994: The views of teachers and children* (Mason, 1995). Even though the report only deals briefly, and somewhat tangentially, with teachers' "philosophies" it does enough to indicate the continued existence of many of the aforementioned ideological themes and, when placed alongside the views of teachers gathered from elsewhere (see, for example, Armour, 1997; Armour and Jones, 1998), provides a reasonable picture from which some broad generalisations can be made.

Despite a growing number of PE teachers incorporating health-related justifications as a central ideological underpinning for the subject, in the late 1990s PE has been experiencing a significant shift back towards a renewed emphasis upon team games and sport (so-called "traditional" PE). References in recent government policy statements (see, for example, DCMS, 2000) — to the importance of sport in schools — suggests that the removal of obligatory involvement among older pupils in team games in Curriculum 2000 will do little to alter this trend.

It is abundantly clear, then, that there is a gulf between what academics have to say about the nature and purposes of PE and PE teachers' views about what they should be trying to do. The gulf is more obvious in certain respects than others. For PE teachers the process is far more practically oriented, impressionistic and reactive than the kind of abstract philosophising commonly associated with professional philosophers. Academics can be expected to develop the kind of abstract philosophy that attempts to bring PE into line with other elements of the curriculum by developing an "educational" rationale for physical activity based around achieving similar goals, albeit by different means. PE teachers, on the other hand, appear to arrive at their "philosophies" in response to their intuitions, or habituses, blended with the constraints of their practical situations.

Several features of the everyday "philosophies" of PE teachers, such as the overt emphasis upon enjoyment, the unusual justification for "options", the emphasis upon sports performance (presumably one of the things that discourages some pupils), amongst other things, suggested that PE teachers perceived PE as somehow *different* from the rest of the curriculum. Theirs were very special kinds of "philosophy" characterised by degrees of localism, particularism and subjectivity that stands in marked contrast to what one finds in other areas of the National Curriculum and, indeed, from what OFSTED might demand.

That skill acquisition featured as one of the few overtly "educational" goals of PE teachers' "philosophies" is not altogether surprising, for it is what one would expect with common-sense "philosophies"; PE teachers seldom, if ever, sit down and think their philosophies through, so to speak. Nothing constrains PE teachers to think their "philosophies" through systematically and identify links between the differing aspects thereof. Consequently, they remain a "mish-mash" characterized by preferred and ideological conceptions. On the other hand, a great deal constrains teachers to fashion their thoughts to match the "necessities" of practice and their habitual preferences.

Nothing, perhaps, lends more weight to the view that their "philosophies" or, rather, their ideologies have as much to do with practical constraints as ideological commitment than teachers' acceptance of and support for the dramatic growth of examinable PE.

Here and elsewhere, the views of PE teachers seemed formed, more-or-less substantially, by perceptions of practical constraints — by the compelling nature of context rather than the impact of abstract theorising on the part of teachers. Whereas academics are constrained to "iron out" the inconsistencies in their justifications, PE teachers are not constrained so to do. Indeed, if anything, PE teachers are constrained not to "iron out" inconsistencies. They experience many aspects of their working lives, and lives in general for that matter, as discrete and somewhat immediate elements to be dealt with in the here and now rather than to be considered further on reflection.

Why, then, do PE teachers think the ways they do? How might one satisfactorily explain or account for their kind of views? In Chapter 5, I will attempt to explain how the "philosophies" held by PE teachers and their underlying ideologies can best be explained in terms of the networks of social relationships — or figurations — of which they are a part.

5

Making Sense of Physical Education Teachers' "Philosophies"

In the preceding chapters I have suggested that PE teachers' views on the nature and purposes of their subject — their "philosophies" — possess several noteworthy characteristics. Far from being *philosophical* in nature (in the sense of being abstract, detached and rational conceptualisations of PE), teachers' notions of PE are, in fact, quite *ideological*; that is to say, they are made up of more-or-less mythical ideas regarding physical education. Indeed, teachers' "philosophies" appear somewhat confused, at times contradictory, rather impressionistic and only partly formed, *preferred* views of PE that tend to be far more involved than detached in nature. As such, PE teachers' "philosophies" are prone to being value-laden, practical outlooks that represent an amalgam of various ideologies — featuring what I have termed sporting, health and academic ideologies — and prominent amongst which are concerns with enjoyment, sports performance, fitness and professional status.

It was noteworthy from the study that sport in general, and team games in particular, were seen as a sine qua non of the PE curriculum for many, if not all, PE teachers, no matter where the balance point of their ideological leanings lay. Regardless of which conceptions of the subject achieve pre-eminence at the level of academic or professional debate, it is apparent that one particular ideology endures at the level of PE teaching, that of sport. In this vein, teachers in the study tended to possess a distinctive view of PE — one that was quite *particular* and rather *subjective* as well as less serious than one might expect. Whilst aspects of their ideologies could be said to approximate to the conventional academic conceptions of PE (such as the moral benefits of sport in an educational context and sport being a valued cultural practice) this was as much serendipitous as it was deliberate. Where it appeared deliberate (for example, academic justifications for PE), it was more likely to be the consequence of an *ex post facto* seizure of suitable justifications — in order to bolster preferred ideological views and customary practices — than a matter of inferential reasoning[1] per se. In this manner, many teachers seemed to have somewhat teleological (one might even say, functionalist) perceptions of PE; as if, in other words, they were saying "If PE did not have positive social and educational purposes or functions to fulfil it would not exist".

In this chapter I want, then, to explore how, from a sociological perspective, one might begin to explain these "philosophical" (or, more accurately, ideological) orientations of PE teachers. I want to suggest that, instead of being premised upon abstract analytical reasoning as such, PE teachers' "philosophies" are typically grounded in their figurations — two particularly salient features of which are their *habituses* (the various values and associated predispositions that suffuse their lives) and their *contexts* (including teachers' perceptions of interest and constraint). Consequently, it will be argued that, if we want to understand why teachers come to think and believe as they do about the nature and purposes of PE and, indeed, their everyday practice, then we need to explore the networks of social relations — or figurations — of which they are a part. It is claimed here that it is not possible to explain the thoughts and practices of PE teachers in terms of the freely and rationally chosen beliefs and behaviours of individuals independent of other individuals and groups — in the past as well as the present. Rather, they can only be explained, "if one takes into account the compelling forces" (Elias; cited in Mennell and Goudsblom, 1998, p. 118) that are a consequence of teachers' interdependence with a range of other people and groups of people.

For ease of explanation, I will divide the analysis up into the three dimensions — the personal, the local and the national — that, it is held, constitute the multilevel, multidimensional "game" or process of education.

PE Teachers in their Figurations: The Personal Dimension

To view PE teachers' "philosophies" merely in the context of their immediate circumstances would be to make a significant error.

---

[1] Of the kind that frequently appears assumed — either implicitly or explicitly — in the writings of various PE philosophers and teacher-trainers (Green, 1998, 2000).

People's thoughts and behaviours tend to bear the hallmark of past as well as present experiences. The figurations of which individuals have been, and continue to be, a part have long-term significance for their identities and habituses. Thus, the networks of relationships in which teachers have been involved previously can be seen to have as much potential significance for their thoughts and practices as those in which they are currently involved, since both are likely to affect their disposition towards PE.

PE Teachers' Biographies and Sporting Identities

A good deal of international research over the last decade or so[2] suggests that the biographies of prospective PE teachers, and particularly their own childhood experiences of sport and school PE, have an ongoing influence on their values, thoughts and practices. In terms of explaining *why* PE teachers think the way they do about their subject, it is important to remind ourselves that their emotional ties to, and identification with, sport forms what Elias would describe as "a deep-anchorage in the personality structure" (or habitus) of young sportsmen and sportswomen. It becomes a significant dimension of their individual and collective identities and one which "cannot easily be shaken off" (Elias; cited in Mennell and Goudsblom, 1998, p. 251), not least because what people value tends to be shaped by what they have experience of as well as competence in.

In line with the findings of a number of authors writing on the theme of the socialisation of PE teachers (see, for example, Dewar and Lawson, 1984; O'Bryant, O'Sullivan and Raudensky, 2000), for many teachers in my study (see Green, 2000) valuing sport was a pervasive and enduring influence being, as it was, central to many of their lives and identities ("I love sport and all the different activities"). Associated with this, experiencing success in sport led to them valuing opportunities for sporting competition. This "love of sport" had been influential at the outset of their teaching careers — in terms of their original orientation or "subjective warrant" (Curtner-Smith, 2001; Dewar and Lawson, 1984; Lawson, 1983a, 1983b;

[2] See, for example, Armour, 1997, Brown, 1999, Evans and Williams, 1989 in the UK; Chen and Ennis, 1996, Lawson, 1983a, 1983b, Placek *et al.*, 1995, Schempp, 1989, Templin and Schempp, 1989, Tsangaridou and Siedentop, 1995 in the USA; and Macdonald, Kirk and Braiuka, 1999 in Australia.

O'Bryant *et al.*, 2000;) – and continued to be so, regardless of their age or gender.

Thus, teachers' "philosophies" (in sociological terms, their ideologies) and, for that matter, their reasons for entering PE – what has been referred to as the anticipatory phase of occupational socialisation (Dewar and Lawson, 1984; Lawson, 1988; O'Bryant *et al.*, 2000) – are best understood in terms of teachers' habitus; in short, their "second nature" (Elias, 1978). Their biographies, and particularly their early and profound attachments to sport, had developed in them a typical orientation towards PE, and particularly competitive sport. The responses of these teachers regarding their biographies lent weight to a conceptualisation of childhood and youth as "the main 'transmission belt' for the development of habitus" (van Krieken, 1998, p. 156), habituses which have come to characterise social groups such as PE teachers. Thus, as Dewar and Lawson (1984) and Placek *et al.* (1995), among others, have observed, the sporting biographies of prospective teachers and their PE experiences as pupils act, in effect, to socialise them into particular views regarding the nature and purposes of the subject: into particular "philosophies" or, more exactly, ideologies.

It is somewhat unsurprising, then, to find teachers inclined towards replicating (because they feel more comfortable with them) "traditional" approaches to "traditional" curricula. Thus, the sport- and games-oriented PE programme associated with so-called "traditional" PE has had a degree of self-replication built in to it and, as such, has become to a significant degree self-fulfilling. Given that a self-selecting and self-replicating process seems to be at work, it was not surprising to find many teachers committed to "traditional" PE and the values underpinning it.

Lawson coined the phrase "subjective warrant" to refer to the various ways in which "a person's perception of the requirements of and benefits of work in a given profession weighed against self-assessments of aspiration and competence" (Lawson, 1983a, p. 13; cited in Curtner-Smith, 2001). One form of subjective warrant, Lawson suggests, is a "coaching orientation": that is to say, the desire to *coach* school sport, and particularly school sports teams. The other prominent form of subjective warrant is, according to Lawson, a "teaching orientation", wherein the would-be teacher's main concern is with *teaching* curricular PE (Curtner-Smith, 2001;

emphasis added). Coaching sport is supposedly seen as a "career contingency" to would-be teachers with such a warrant. Whilst, from a figurational perspective, such a distinction represents something of a "false dichotomy", my own research goes part way to supporting Lawson's (1983a) claim that many trainee teachers "wished to become physical education teachers mainly because they wanted to coach school sports teams" (Curtner-Smith, 2001, p. 83). In this vein, my research added weight to the view (Lawson, 1983a; Curtner-Smith, 2001) that teacher-trainees with a strong sporting ideology tend to focus whenever and wherever they can on coaching sports rather than teaching physical activities in PE.

Professional Socialisation: Teacher Training
I have noted the significance of PE and sporting experiences for teachers — both in terms of their initial choices of career as well as their more-or-less unwitting adoption of particular PE "philosophies" or, rather, ideologies. What is also noteworthy is the seemingly relative insignificance for PE teachers' "philosophies" of professional training. It is clear that PE teachers do not arrive for teacher training as tabulae rasae. Rather, they arrive with particular dispositions, or *habituses*. By the time many teachers reach the training stage they have, more-or-less wittingly, become accustomed to associating PE primarily with "sport in schools". There is a tendency towards conservatism present which manifests itself in the passing on of skills-oriented and sport-dominated curricula. Teacher-trainees and "beginning" teachers (McCormack, 1997) are, according to Placek *et al.* (1995), oriented toward "reproducing and preserving the physical education they have experienced" (p. 248), not least because, as Lawson (1983a) and Curtner-Smith (2001) have observed, many trainees enter PE with the hope and expectation of *coaching* and coaching sport (what Lawson terms a coaching-oriented subjective warrant).

Against this background, a number of comments from teachers in my study (Green, 2000) confirmed the findings of others in this regard (see, for example, Evans, 1992; McCormack, 1997; Placek *et al.*, 1995), thereby lending credence to the claim that initial teacher training (ITT) has little impact on the already established "philosophies" and practices of would-be PE teachers. Indeed, and in line with the observation of Curtner-Smith (2001, p. 82) among others, teaching practice tends to "confirm [teacher-trainees'] beliefs and values rather than [act] as a source of modification".

In the same way that the significance of theoretical definitions of PE for teachers' "philosophies" and practices is frequently exaggerated, so there is also a tendency to overemphasise the significance of training in this regard. In this context, the negligible impact of professional socialisation on the ideologies of prospective PE teachers is particularly evident. The aspect of ITT that appears to have a more substantial impact on PE teachers' "philosophies" is, unsurprisingly, teaching practice — that is to say, the time spent actually teaching PE in schools under the tutelage of an established teacher-mentor. As Curtner-Smith (2001, p. 82) observes:

> interactions with significant people [such, we might add, as established PE teachers] lead to an understanding of what it means to be a physical education teacher.

For teachers themselves, then, it is likely that "practice" may be perceived as significantly more influential than "training". Notwithstanding this observation, in one very broad sense teacher training (as with education per se) can clearly be seen to matter or, rather, to make a difference. This is the sense in which the difference between a qualified teacher and a non-teacher is that the former has been trained/educated to teach. In relation to this, and primarily in order to gain academic or professional qualification (and licence), people change or amend their views, learn the things they are obliged to learn, even believe the things they need to believe — or, at least, appear to do all of these things — in order to achieve a desired outcome: in this case, teach PE. However, at a lower level of generality, education appears to make no difference; that is to say, the difference between teachers with varying "philosophies" is unlikely to be explainable in terms of their training. Indeed, the development in prospective teachers' thinking — that might appear to take place during the period of their training — does not necessarily signify a substantive change of values, beliefs and attitudes on their part at a deeper psychological level. Neither, for that matter, does it necessarily help explain teachers' behaviours. This is precisely because it may be more apparent than real. When viewed sociologically, what people think, as well as the behaviours they are inclined towards, are best explained in terms of a blend of more deeply seated values, beliefs and attitudes and the context in which they operate. In particular, what tend to make a substantive difference to practice (as opposed to theory or philosophy) are differences in people's *circumstances*.

Professional Socialisation: "On the Job Experiences"
The socially constructed nature of PE teachers' "philosophies" is, of course, a process and, as such, does not cease on completion of teacher training. Making sense of PE teachers' "philosophies" requires appreciation of the ways in which prospective teachers' sporting and PE backgrounds interact at one level with their occupational socialisation but also with broader professional and socio-political contexts, as well as the prevailing ideologies found therein. Thus, what physical educationalists think, as well as what they do, may — partially at least — be explained in terms of dealing with the constraints of the day-to-day practice of teaching ("I've learnt a lot actually on the job ... I've learnt a heck of a lot here") or, as Fejgin (1995) puts it, "solving functional problems".

It was apparent from my own study that teachers' "philosophies" were processual: they appeared to have amended their views and practices, by degrees, in accordance with their perceptions of surrounding contextual constraints. The comments of one teacher offered a neat illustration of the manner in which the common-sense (sporting) ideology of some teachers developed to incorporate the constraints of practice as they experienced them:

> I thought that being a PE teacher was about getting these wonderful teams together... But then I realised that not all children are like that... over the years you get more realistic, so you look more at their individual levels and you just try to push that child at their level.

Several teachers suggested that their practice reflected in part an appreciation of "changing times" and, in particular, what Roberts (1996b) has referred to as "youth's new condition":

> I've probably moved with the times...when I first started...football was the main thing everywhere... I just lived and breathed football... I found, really, that I wasn't catering for all the kids in my school.

In this regard, it was evident that the more common reasons cited for developments in practice as well as "philosophies" had to do with reactions to the context in which teachers found themselves teaching (rather than professional initiatives or literature): that is to say, constraints operating at the local level of the school:

> At 21, when you first start teaching, you've not really had a lot of experience of working with kids...at 21 you come in and you want everybody to get in netball teams, you want everybody sprinting down, and everybody throwing their discus miles. And then you stop and you think, "Well, it's not working!"

PE Teachers in their Figurations: The Local Dimension

In this section I intend to explore those aspects of PE teachers' figurations – at what might be called the local level of day-to-day practice in schools – that appear to influence their "philosophies": that is to say, those aspects of what O'Donnell (1981, p. 564) refers to as "the culture of the workplace" which "generates or reinforces values, beliefs and normative attitudes which contribute to the general stock of assumptions or knowledge...of given societies or groups".

One point that is worthy of note at the outset is the extent to which, as the network of relationships in which PE teachers are enmeshed becomes ever more complex, their chains of interdependency lengthen to incorporate not only their pupils and fellow teachers, but also the pupils' parents, local sporting and community groups and so forth, as well as professional interest groups representing PE teachers.

Salient among the many and varied local constraints identified by teachers in my study were those posed by "significant others" (particularly head teachers, heads of departments – as well as more established PE colleagues – the pupils themselves and their parents) and local conventions and traditions (such as the inheritance of sporting and religious traditions). In the first instance, I will explore what might be seen – with regard to professional relationships at least – as the epicentre of schools, namely head teachers and senior managers, and move "outwards" through colleagues, pupils and parents.

Significant Others: Senior Colleagues

Unsurprisingly, most of the teachers in my study perceived themselves as more-or-less "at the mercy" of the expectations of their head teacher, their heads of departments (HoDs) and senior colleagues. Teachers viewed head teachers as presenting a particularly significant constraining influence on PE:

> I've got quite disheartened with it…[the] lack of opportunities…I just wish [the] school [management] would put more importance on it [PE].

In concrete terms, the pressures on teachers from head teachers and senior managers often took the form of anticipation of sporting success for their school:

> Fixtures take precedence for us because that's what he [the head teacher] judges as our exam results… "How many did you play? How many did you win?"

Many teachers (and especially HoDs) commented upon what they perceived as their head teacher's view of the role of PE in their school, and many commented upon the "head's" inclination to "interfere", directly or indirectly. Several recognised that the head teachers were themselves operating in contexts that constrained their behaviour — whether in the form, for example, of government policy statements or the internal market in education that had emerged from previous legislation ("I think it [league tables] is steering the whole of the school!"). Indeed, many teachers, but especially the HoDs, often appeared aware of the "necessity" of exploiting sport in what they deemed to be the school's interest ("basically we want to get more parents to send kids here rather than send them to…"). This concern for the prestige of the school in the context of a quasi-educational market (Penney and Evans, 1999) was particularly evident with regard to the constraints teachers felt themselves to be under vis-à-vis provision of extra-curricular PE.

For many teachers, HoDs and senior colleagues within their departments were an additional layer of constraining influence to contend with, either directly or indirectly ("a lot [of what you do] depends on your Head of Department"). Many younger teachers in the study felt particularly constrained by being "a junior member of staff" ("I wouldn't dare suggest it… I've got no say, I'm just a 'pleb' … I'm just here to teach"). Despite this, it was noticeable that the power relations experienced by the teachers were neither linear (that is to say, they were frequently not a straightforward effect of the power consequences often viewed as inherent in ostensibly hierarchical line-management relationships) nor did they constrain the teachers to face in a single direction. HoDs, as well as ordinary members of those departments, were also constrained by relationships with other teachers. One HoD, for example, commented thus:

> Sometimes I think the philosophy of what you want to do does get pushed by the wayside with practicalities…there always seems to be a pull towards everybody's specialisms or ideals of what they think… and, of course, different people enjoy different things and feel that certain things should be included in the timetable, so it's a constant readjustment of…where the emphasis should lie.

In addition to the complex, multidirectional network of relations experienced by teachers in their schools and departments, the figurations of which the teachers were a part evidently included groups of people beyond the immediate confines of the school setting. The interdependency networks of PE teachers do not end at the staff room or gym door. Local dimensions of the networks incorporate the impact of pupils and parents on what PE teachers do, as well as what they think about what they do.

Significant Others: Pupils

In addition to the more immediate influence of colleagues, teachers felt constrained by what they perceived as the expectations of the pupils ("our after-school activities are mainly team based…our children will not come unless they are in a team") — as well as their parents — in relation to sport and sporting competition. Many teachers commented on their perceptions of the pupils' expectations in general:

> We are all aware we do too much games…but nothing ever happens about it… Because that's what the kids enjoy.

It is worthy of note that the constraining impact of pupils' expectations, and concomitant behaviour, was particularly pertinent for those teaching in schools in relatively deprived areas. Here, the "type of kids", in conjunction with the area in which the school was located, were offered as especially irresistible influences on teachers' thoughts and practices. Teachers who perceived the pupils in their schools as being underprivileged frequently described them as potentially difficult to manage. When they spoke in terms of their "philosophies" and their practices, these teachers made frequent reference, for example, to the pupils' likes and dislikes as well as their expectations of, abilities in and commitment to PE:

> [There is a] mismatch... [National Curriculum Physical Education] doesn't work for a large percent[age] of our kids... [It] was implemented...without any consideration [of] the type of kids we've got, the area we've got, what sports are available for kids in and around the area and, basically, what the parents want.

The "type" of pupils not only influenced what some PE teachers considered they were trying to achieve, but also affected their views on what constituted a satisfactory outcome ("sometimes I'm just pleased at the end of the lesson if they've just done it"), for, as Curtner-Smith (2001) observes, pupil lack of interest has a particularly negative impact upon teachers' perceptions of their role. On the whole, then, those teachers in underprivileged catchment areas saw themselves as what might justifiably be termed "outsiders" (see Scotson and Elias, 1994)[3] looking in on mainstream PE. They tended to be acutely aware of the impact their schools' catchment areas had upon their "philosophies" and practices. Thus, it was a feature of various teachers' comments that their "philosophies" had, in line with their practice, changed somewhat as a consequence of teaching in a disadvantaged school:

> My view has changed since I've been here...I found...that I wasn't really catering for all the kids in my school and when I started talking to some of my colleagues and some of the heads of departments...they also felt the same thing.

Teachers in schools where participation was not a major problem often had little in the way of empathy for colleagues in more deprived areas. Indeed, comparisons were sometimes made — by these "insiders" looking out — contrasting rough schools with suc-

---

[3] In Eliasian terms, the situation of PE teachers — at both the local and national levels — bears comparison with the Scotson and Elias (1994) notion of "outsider" groups in relation to those who might be considered more "established". Eminently accusable in relation to a range of concerns stretching from sporting performance of national teams through moral awareness/character development to the "health of the nation", the "philosophies" of teachers in the present study suggest that many of the claims made of teachers in relation to their "radical", "progressive" (Evans, 1990) or other such views on the nature and purposes of their subject could only be found "among a very small minority: a 'minority of the worst'" (Elias; cited in Mennell and Goudsblom, 1998, p. 250).

cessful sports programmes in other regions and those who were "failing" locally. In this regard, established teachers with "traditional" views on PE were frequently inclined to caricature those they saw as non-traditionalists in a manner that served to reinforce any inclination that these "outsiders" may have had to see themselves as failing in some way.

The tension between official expectations (see, for example, QCA, 1999), the reality of teachers' situations as they perceived them and aspects of their "philosophies" was neatly illustrated in a passage from an interview with a teacher from a relatively deprived school in a new town. She made clear her commitment to encouraging lifelong participation and "activity choice" and added that, at her school, they offered more choice than NCPE appeared to allow for. She added:

> And I know that's not fulfilling [the National Curriculum] but…they come every week…that's what they want to do and that keeps them happy. And having the choice makes some of the ones that wouldn't particularly want to do it, do it.

In this regard, it was evident that in many teachers' eyes a (and frequently *the*) major constraint on their practice as well as their "philosophies", was the issue of class management and control ("[it's] control rather than teaching too often") and that such concerns were immediate and all-pervasive ("[we're] just pressurised… [if he does not] want to do it you can't make him"). Various teachers acknowledged that their PE programmes as well as those of other teachers were heavily influenced by pragmatism rather than principle and that, in this respect, their "philosophies" as such tended to be "based on what works" ("some people [teachers] play football all the way through to 'avoid hassle'").

Both female and male teachers perceived differing contexts constraining them to adapt their teaching, especially with regard to the apparent reluctance of older girls towards PE:

> By Year 10, quite a few of my girls aren't into playing…games any more and particularly the lower [ability]…ones, and they absolutely love doing aerobics… They would give me so much more effort throughout the year if they were doing aerobics the whole time… So, I'm really torn between keeping the games going because [some] are good, but what about all these others that are only giving me 60%?

Associated with, and working in much the same direction as, the constraints associated with the perceived threat of pupil disaffection, were the expectations of parents.

Significant Others: Parents

According to a large number of teachers in my study, parents were an increasingly constraining factor. Parents were said to be crucial in some areas because, as one teacher succinctly put it, they are viewed by teachers as likely to say, "My son doesn't have to do this if he doesn't want to". In particular, parents were seen as taking more interest in competitive sport than recreational exercise: "If there were teams involved or competitions or prizes they [parents] come in droves". Parents of pupils at relatively affluent schools were perceived by teachers to be particularly keen on competitive sports and especially team games. Ironically, however (given the relative failure they often experienced themselves, as young people, in sport and particularly team games), parents from lower socio-economic groups were also viewed as advocates of competitive sport and games-based curricula as well as extra-curricular PE.

It is hardly surprising, then, as Penney and Harris (1997, p. 48) suggest, that "in conditions of competition between schools for pupils, PE teachers may be encouraged to respond to parents' views". Many teachers held that parents' expectations were largely in line with those of the pupils themselves. Parents and pupils, it was claimed, expected to be in matches: "We get a lot of flack...from parents of children who are not up to team standard". A previous Minister for Sport's commitment to "changing the ethos of school sport, and involving parents more" (Davies, 1999, p. 40) suggests that the constraints operating at the national and local level of their figurations will constrain PE teachers even more, in the near future, towards a sporting ideology.

The Inheritance of Tradition

Whilst there are a number of significant practical constraints shaping the practice of PE teachers, and thus the make-up of the PE curriculum, it is important to recognise that PE teachers, head teachers and governors *in the past*, as well as the present, have influenced the context in which teachers currently work. Each generation of PE teachers inherits a PE world that is processual and, as such, reflects the existence of widespread continuities alongside degrees of change. Thus, the ongoing influence of custom and practice was apparent in the comments of many teachers in the study. A female teacher commented that "When I came here it was what they did, so I've carried on what was already established". Others pointed to the logistical constraints ("It's such an organisational nightmare trying to avoid all the matches") or the potential conflict situations facing anyone considering pressing for change:

> If I suddenly change things — "Why? Why?" It's not worth the hassle. These things have always been done the same…I get the impression that's why we do it.

It was evident that most teachers perceived their schools as having some form of sporting tradition, which it was, at least in part, the function of extra-curricular PE to maintain ("when I do extra-curricular here we have a lot of pressure on us to have [good] team results…so fixtures take a precedence for us"). This appeared to be particularly the case for those departments within schools in which sporting success was seen as an especially valuable aspect of the "marketing" of the school. Even where teachers appeared keen to "branch out", so to speak, they were inevitably more-or-less constrained by the relative dominance of a sporting ideology at the school and/or department levels ("We do a lot of games. But I feel that the [pupils] shouldn't just be [given] team games, we have to do a wide range of games").

It is worth reminding ourselves, however, that pressure also surfaces from within, for teachers have their own expectations of sporting involvement and success among the pupils ("there's no pressure here to be successful, but it's a personal thing — if we do well we feel great about it"). Some traditions appeared to constrain teachers to provide what amounted to *ex post facto* justifications for their practices — "philosophies" that were, in effect, "bolted-on" to what they already did without having felt the need to provide justifications of that sort. This did not, however, prevent the teachers concerned appearing to believe the rhetoric themselves.

The Gender Dimension to PE Teachers' Figurations

One particularly important aspect of PE teachers' figurations at both the personal and local levels, but which manifests itself most clearly on the latter plane, is that of gender. It was apparent that the "philosophies" and ostensible practices of many PE teachers in this study continued to reflect degrees of gender stereotyping. In this regard, the constraints of practice frequently served to reinforce rather than to challenge the attitudes and predispositions characteristic of teachers' habituses. Indeed, the views of teachers in the present study tended to support the claim that NCPE and recent developments at the national level (Waddington *et al.*, 1998) have reinforced rather than challenged or undermined traditional gender segregation and stereotypes at the local level.

Whilst the views and practices of some men and women ran counter to the dominant pattern, it was evident that men remained more likely than women to hold stereotypical views regarding the norms of boys' and girls' PE. It is important to note, nonetheless, that various female teachers also held quite stereotypical views regarding gender norms, as illustrated by their marked reluctance towards the outdoor and adventurous activities area (Waddington *et al.*, 1998). In this regard, it was evident that female teachers were themselves implicated in some forms of constraint in PE and sport along gender lines (Colwell, 1999). It was noticeable that where teachers' intuitive views had been reinforced or challenged, this frequently appeared to have been so, at least in part, on the basis of the constraining influence of experiencing particular circumstances, such as having to teach opposite-sex groups or having relatively positive experiences of teaching particular forms of dance, such as rock-and-roll.

It is also important to note that there was no single set of norms regarding girls' and boys' PE. Rather, there were by degrees differing norms within differing PE departments and frequently, and unsurprisingly, among clusters of teachers in those departments. Nonetheless, among the disparities there were relatively clear patterns that suggested that, whilst not all male teachers shared similar views, gender-stereotypical views were more evident among male than female teachers of PE. In short, the "philosophies" and professed practices of PE teachers in this study reinforced the impression that "the teaching of PE continues in many respects to reproduce rather than to challenge, gender stereotypes" (Waddington *et al.*, 1998, p. 44). Indeed, the tendency of PE teachers, especially established male teachers, to resort to pseudo-educational rationales in support of their "philosophies" and practices appeared "indicative of the amount and strength of resistance to change" (Waddington *et al.*, 1998, p. 44).

PE Teachers in their Figurations: The National Dimension

An adequate appreciation of ideological developments within PE over time — including contemporary views on the nature and purposes of PE — requires an account of broader sociopolitical influences that have shaped the development of the subject in school, as well as the habituses of PE teachers. A number of major changes in the world of education in recent years have had significant implications for PE, not least because of their interconnections with broader developments in other spheres, such as sport. Given the relatively detailed coverage these topics have received elsewhere (see, for example, Penney and Evans, 1997, 1998, 1999), I intend merely to touch upon three salient aspects of the national dimension of PE teachers' figurations: the NCPE, OFSTED and governmental interest in general, and the sports lobby.

Government, the Sports Council (Sport England) and the Sports Lobby

A feature of recent government policy ("Brooking talks on sport", 1999; Davies, 1999; DCMS, 2000; DNH, 1995) has been an expectation that schools will increasingly make use of external sports agencies, in the form of coaches, clubs and courses. In my study, a number of teachers professed themselves willing, indeed keen, to take advantage of such encouragement to make use of coaches in curricular and extra-curricular PE ("I would love...more coaches to come in"). Many appeared ready to accept the increasing involvement of outside coaches not least for a variety of practical reasons, ranging from widening opportunities to assisting the process of class management. Teachers in the study were also keen to develop "connections with outside clubs" and frequently referred to sports clubs as "something we try and steer people towards". With regard to the development of links between PE departments and sports clubs and sports coaches, government and sporting agencies appear to be pushing at a door already ajar. Indeed, the linking of sport and PE that characterises public policy appears to be widely and uncritically accepted not only beyond but also within the various levels of the PE subject-community, from the Physical Education Association-UK (see, for example, Almond, Harrison and Laws, 1996) through to teachers themselves. The transparent government and Sport England view of sport as the primary focus of PE (Talbot, 1995a, 1995b) is more likely to be confirmed than challenged by the PE subject-community. In relation to this, it is worth noting the role of the media in the transmission of particular ideologies and the manner in which media representations of issues portrayed as appertaining to PE (such as national sporting success and health promotion) act as a fund of common-sense justifications for PE for teachers and, indeed, other interested parties in the subject-community.

OFSTED

The comments of teachers in the study suggested that high on the agendas of OFSTED inspectors visiting their departments had been "standards of achievement". This seemed to he reflected in the particular interest, not to say preoccupation, of OFSTED — as measured by their comments in reports upon individual schools, as well as their summary report on PE nationwide (OFSTED, 1998) — with "skill development", "major games", "representative honours" and examinations in PE. The impression one forms of OFSTED's preference for sports performance — over "activity choice" and recreational activities — is reinforced by numerous comments in their reports to schools. It is an impression mirrored in a comment — regarding developments in curricular PE — in their summary report: "A move away from the 'recreational activities' and 'activity choice' approach is also raising achievement levels in Key Stage 4" (OFSTED, 1998).

NCPE

It was clear from the comments of teachers that they perceived NCPE as a major constraint on their practice in recent years. A particular feature of teachers' views was their concern with the practicalities of NCPE, in terms of what requirements they were bound to fulfil rather than any ostensible theory or philosophy underlying it. Such a partial understanding of NCPE, in combination with an overriding concern for the practical implications of the development, was illustrated in the following exchange with a female HoD:

> Teacher: To tell you the truth, I haven't really grasped National Curriculum PE...that seems to be a big thing...the individual skills and team skills... As to what's expected, I wouldn't say I was 100% aware of that. I mean, I go in with the view of what I expect to get out of PE and I've got the curriculum in front of me... I've got a knowledge of what's expected of pupils but...I would not go home and study National Curriculum documents!
> KG: So, what are you trying to achieve?
> Teacher: A well-known philosophy [of] working in schools and seeing what staff are doing, rather than looking in documents.

Unsurprisingly, then, a prevailing concern with the practical implications of NCPE was evident among main-grade PE teachers as well as HoDs:

> I know what the National Curriculum is and what you offer and things, *but I've not really gone into...what's behind it and why we're doing it... Obviously I've got my own views* on whether we should be doing this or that [emphases added].

Many PE teachers expressed a predisposition to modify their preferred practice (in accordance with the requirements of NCPE) to the minimum extent permissable. There seemed to be a tendency towards inertia among PE teachers with regard to developments that they perceived as either unnecessary and/or tangential to the day-to-day demands of doing PE vis-à-vis their custom and practice. In this vein, many teachers gave the impression of viewing NCPE as an obstacle course, a series of hoops to jump through, more or less reluctantly: "I just don't feel I need it. I feel it gets in the way; that I have to do certain things to make it [the curriculum], as it were, legal."

Far from being a straightforward reflection of the intended outcomes of NCPE, it seemed that PE teachers had altered little of their customary practice—both in terms of lesson content and teaching methodology—despite the apparent demands of NCPE ("[we] just modify [the] programme...the minimum to get by really"). Thus, PE teachers' primary concern appeared to be managing NCPE in relation to the constraints, as they perceived them, of their particular working situations ("as long as we offer them a game we're alright"). Uppermost in PE teachers' minds seemed to be *adapting to* or, rather, simply *coping with*, the additional demands of NCPE on their day-to-day working lives. It appears, then, that even the advent of a National Curriculum for PE has not brought the ostensibly much sought-after consensus of thought or deed or, to put it another way, of "philosophy" or practice.

It is clear that some of the constraints that PE teachers experience at the local level emanate from developments at the national level. These wider developments — rehearsed extensively elsewhere (see, for example, Penney and Evans, 1997, 1998, 1999) — circumscribe and impact upon the "philosophies" and practices of PE teachers and consequently affect PE as it is experienced by school pupils.

Conclusion

This chapter has sought to establish the socio-genesis of PE teachers' "philosophical" (or, rather, ideological) orientations from a sociological (specifically, figurational) perspective. Starting from the premise that such "philosophies" cannot be adequately explained by studying either the ideas themselves or the teacher him- or herself in isolation, it has been argued that PE teachers' everyday "philosophies", and the underlying ideologies therein, can only be fully understood when teachers are located in the figurations they form with each other — as inescapably *interdependent* people. Two salient dimensions of the figurations of PE teachers are identified as their deeply rooted attachments and associated convictions (for example, towards the value of sport) and their practice of PE or, more precisely, the constraints circumscribing their practice.

In accordance with the findings of Lawson (1983a, 1983b), among others (see, for example, Curtner-Smith, 1995; Curtner-Smith and Meek, 2000), my study provided evidence to suggest that the way teachers thought about PE had been shaped by their deep-seated predispositions (or habitus) — in particular, towards sport and PE. Nonetheless, whilst habitus is formed in early life, it remains susceptible to development as networks of relationships become ever more complex and compelling, especially in and around the world of work. In this regard, PE teachers are increasingly related to a large number, and wide range, of other people at one and the same time — not least because they are surrounded by people connected in one way or another to the subject matter of PE (such as other teachers, parents, pupils, coaches, representatives of various sporting lobbies, Government and the media). It is somewhat unsurprising, therefore, to find that PE teachers' "philosophies" — as well as their practices—represent something of a compromise. PE teachers respond to the immediate pressures of their working situation as involved participants in the "hurly-burly" of teaching and view the attendant constraints as more *urgent* if not more important. In this sense, PE teachers' views on their subject frequently appear more *reactive* than *proactive*. This leads me to conclude, along with Evans (1992, p. 243), that where "tension" exists "between the operational ideology and the fundamental ideology" this tends, on the part of teachers, to lead to "some modification in the latter".

The personal and local dimensions to figurations are intimately related to developments at the national level, even though these are less transparent to teachers and their influence on teachers' "philosophies" is less obvious. As well as serving to re-prioritise sport and team games within the PE curriculum, government and Sport England policy statements and pronouncements in recent years have further encouraged an already strong sporting culture within schools. Thus, the predominantly sporting ideological view of PE represents not only a "privileging" of sport over physical activity but also a "hardening" of a hierarchy of activities well established within PE, which continues to feature sport and games at the apex (Penney and Evans, 1999). The emphasis upon sport and team games from both within and without the subject-community of PE allows some teachers to maintain preferred views of PE (as oriented towards sport and performance) whilst, at the same time, constraining the development of alternative conceptions of the nature and purposes of the subject. It is worth remembering, however, that the extent to which these constraints are, in effect, hindering many (and especially male) teachers from pursuing their "ideal" PE provision or, rather, providing a fund of "handy" justifications for what, in reality, amount to their preferred practices — sport and team games — remains an open question.

Whilst PE teachers cannot be described as a homogenous group, neither for that matter are they heterogeneous as such. Indeed, many appear to share similar habituses at the personal level and all are constrained by similar circumstances at the local and national dimensions of their figurations. Hence, we are left with the impression of a group habitus in the sense of a shared fund of common-sense understandings and justificatory ideas or ideologies at the local level — what might be termed "articles of faith" — which PE teachers share with each other in the course of their normal, everyday working lives. With this point in mind, it is worthy of note that the largely normative views of their subject that teachers internalise are, to some extent, transmitted by these teachers to future teachers while the latter are pupils experiencing school and college PE. Hence, the likelihood that PE teachers' outlook on PE will remain to a greater or lesser extent tied to "yesterday's social reality". The particular networks of relationships that PE teachers inhabit make particular interpretations of PE more likely than others. As such, PE teachers' "philosophies" tended to be *practical* — that is to say, "philosophies" that bore the hallmarks of their prior PE and sporting practice and their contemporaneous practical teaching contexts.

From a (figurational) sociological perspective, it is argued that normative views on the nature and purposes of PE in England and Wales must be understood as the (often unintended) outcomes of long-term social developments. PE teachers' figurations are, as with figurations per se, historically produced and reproduced networks of interdependence. Sporting ideologies have been passed on from one generation of PE teachers to the next. The "traditional" games-based curriculum that became a feature of the nascent secondary-school PE after the World War II was, itself, an imitation of public-school curricula of a century earlier (Kirk, 1992a). Having said that, in common with all social processes, PE teachers' figurations are in flux and the evident processes of academicisation and professionalisation have made their mark on the subject-community of PE. Unsurprisingly, therefore, there is evidence that the constraints of their figurations are impacting upon their "philosophies" and practices, at least in curricular PE. Some of the changes associated with the changing figurations have been relatively rapid and have been associated with more-or-less prominent ideologies (for example, the process of academicisation in PE, including the dramatic growth of examinations) whilst others have been more gradual (the emergence of HRE). The social processes of medicalisation (of life in general, as well as sport and PE in particular) and professionalisation may well prove to be the motors that drive psychological change further among PE teachers in the directions of health and academic ideologies. Nevertheless, it is noteworthy that, whilst some of these changes appear likely to be substantial and long lasting, they are occurring alongside a strong element of continuity, not least in the form of the pre-eminence of a sporting ideology in the everyday "philosophies" of PE teachers.

6

Conclusion

The ample literature of the last twenty years or so, theorising education from philosophical and pedagogical perspectives, frequently incorporates an implicit assumption that the primary purpose of education is the transformation of young people's thinking in a manner likely to enhance their understanding of the world in which they live. This, in turn, is expected to bring about the realisation of a sine qua non of liberal educational philosophy: the emergence of the autonomous adult who would, *inter alia*, be subject to the dictate of reason. A premise of a good deal of educational theory is that it can be expected to have much the same impact upon teachers' thinking and practice. In the case of PE it is frequently assumed that teachers themselves are duty-bound to share such a perspective on educational philosophy. But what is the evidence that teachers reflect upon PE in a manner that bears any resemblance to the kind of abstract reasoning usually associated with philosophical theory itself? For that matter, what is the empirical evidence to suggest that teachers' views or "philosophies" are affected by their education or teacher training or, for that matter, by *any* theorising at *any* level?

In attempting to make sense of the relationship between PE teachers' "philosophies" and the ideologies underpinning these, this book has sought to identify and examine what teachers themselves, rather than academics or teacher-trainers, think PE is about — not, it should be noted, in the belief that these "philosophies" might be taken to be self-evidently "true" but, rather, in an attempt to construct a more systematic understanding of PE teachers' views of their subject "in the belief that greater understanding will enhance our capacity to exercise control" (Dunning, 1999, p. 240) over an important aspect of young people's educational experiences.

In order to achieve this, I have attempted to explore PE teachers' habituses as part of their lived reality: that is to say, the various predispositions that suffuse their personal and professional lives as well as the inevitable constraints provided by the particular circumstances they experience. In (figurational) sociological terms, these predispositions and contextual constraints can be viewed as aspects of people's networks of interdependency or figurations. Put another way, the book has taken a figurational approach to making (sociological) sense of PE teachers' "philosophies". This approach — to identifying the ideological themes permeating PE teachers' "philosophies" — has necessitated a shift of focus away from what has hitherto been an undue concentration on the justificatory ideas themselves — the academic philosophies of PE — towards a closer examination of the networks of relationships in which PE teachers, as practitioners, are enmeshed and which form the essential context for understanding their everyday "philosophies". Before saying more about the relationship between PE teachers' thinking and their networks of interdependency (or figurations), I want briefly to summarise, and comment upon, my findings with regard to their "philosophies" per se.

PE Teachers' "Philosophies" and the Ideological Themes therein

Enjoyment

It was apparent that the vast majority, if not all, of the PE teachers in this study (similar to those in Mason's [1995] and Sport England's [2001] research) brought to teaching a taste — passion would not be too strong a word — for physical activity in general and sport in particular. In part, this explains why they appear to place such emphasis upon "enjoyment" as a central feature of their "philosophies". They want youngsters to enjoy what they themselves prize so highly, even though, it is worth noting, enjoyment would not normally be considered a necessary condition of education as such. This is an interesting point, for PE teachers have a distinctive view of their subject, one that is more particular and subjective than one might expect to find with teachers of more "academic" subjects. Indeed, one would expect little sympathy for "enjoyment" as an *aim* of education amongst any other group of educationalists for whom education might even be seen as the very antithesis of "fun". The idea implicit in PE teachers' comments was that, notwithstanding their desire, and claims for, parity of academic and professional esteem, PE teachers see theirs as a less serious subject, one that is, indeed, not really educational in the "standard" or orthodox sense (Reid, 1996a, 1996b).

This notwithstanding, an emotional attachment to sport—together with an ideological commitment to its alleged worth—is only one aspect of PE teachers' emphasis upon enjoyment. To make sense of why enjoyment frequently ranks more highly on the scale of teachers' aims than traditionally highly valued outcomes such as, for example, skill development, one needs to look further than enjoyment as a precondition for continued involvement and commitment to sport, as important as this is. One needs also to appreciate that the context in which PE teachers operate is one in which ensuring participation in and adherence to PE, let alone sport, is an ever-present practical concern. In this respect, it was apparent that in PE teachers' minds enjoyment was often viewed as strongly associated with orderliness in the classroom and, consequently, as something akin to a prerequisite for successful teaching. This was in addition, and prior to, being a feature of lifelong commitment to sport—either for its own sake, for personal and development reasons, or even in the service of active (healthy) lifestyles.

The Ideology of Sport and "Traditional" Team Games
Equally implicit, and frequently explicit, was the perception among PE teachers that the subject of enjoyment should be physical activity generally but sport particularly. Regardless of which conceptions of the subject achieve pre-eminence at the level of academic or professional debate, it is apparent that one particular ideology endures at the level of PE teaching: that of sport. Teachers in the study tended to possess a distinctive view of PE: one that was quite *particular* and rather *subjective* as well as less serious than one might expect. In this vein, the long-standing common-sense ideologies of PE teachers regarding the intrinsic and extrinsic worth of sport to individuals and institutions alike, as well as the emphasis upon sports performance as a central dimension of PE, suffused the comments of virtually all teachers in the study — male and female, young and old. Such ideological commitments to sport, whilst present among all groups of teachers, were most distinct and more thoroughly pervasive in the comments of relatively more established, male PE teachers. Sport in general and team games in particular were seen as a sine qua non of the PE curriculum for

many, if not all, PE teachers regardless of where the balance point of their ideological leanings lay.

The Ideology of Health

PE teachers' responses regarding health and fitness were also particularly interesting. The views of a good many PE teachers were heavily tinted with health-related ideological justifications for PE. Whilst the overriding impression from many teachers' comments was that they believed — at "gut" level — that PE had primarily to do with sport, at the same time they also placed great store by the ability of physical activity and particularly sport to promote individuals' health (both mental and physical, both now and in the future). Alongside, and frequently associated with, the common assumption that the primary aim of PE was enjoyment of those, largely sporting, activities that made up the traditional PE curriculum was the claim that this was beneficial for health reasons. Indeed, health [promotion] was typically described as the major contribution of PE to youngsters' education. It was interesting to note, however, that this was more often on the basis of "lay" understandings of the relationship between health and exercise than health-related justifications espoused in the NCPE or, for that matter, in the theory underpinning HRE. It appeared that a commonsense "paramedical" role for PE had infused many teachers' "philosophies".

"Education for Leisure" and "Sport for All" Ideologies

In line with the claims of Roberts (1996a, 1996b) and Scraton (1992, 1995), it was apparent that the "philosophies" of many teachers in this study incorporated belief in the value to young people of a disposition towards leading physically active, healthy lives. Thus, most teachers' "philosophies" included some commitment to an education for beneficial use of leisure time. Whilst at one time (in the 1970s, for example) this might have been primarily for reasons of social control, in the 1990s it was ostensibly justified primarily on health grounds. Associated with an "education for leisure" ideology was one of "sport for all" — an ideology revolving around the value of lifelong participation in sport for a breadth of personal and social benefits alongside that of health.

It was noteworthy that the ideologies of "education for leisure" and "sport for all" were particularly common among two groups of teachers: those teaching in schools in disadvantaged areas and teachers (almost entirely female) of girls' PE. A significant dimension of these ideologies was teachers' commitment to "activity choice" or "option" PE — a commitment many teachers continued to adhere to despite the constraints of NCPE and OFSTED inspections. It was noteworthy, however, that choice frequently continued to revolve around sport and games, partly for ideological reasons and partly for reasons of pragmatism. Thus, "activity choice" had a tendency to supplement rather than replace "traditional" PE. It was also noticeable that a key aspect of this ideology was teachers' emphasis upon enjoyment as the main outcome of participation. In the light of this ostensible commitment to "choice" and "enjoyment", it is worth observing that the perceived need to accommodate older pupils' preferences was indication of a significant degree of pragmatism in PE teachers' "philosophies".

The Academic Ideology
No matter what else they thought PE should be about, many teachers appeared to feel the need to put some kind of educational "gloss" on their "philosophies" of PE — "philosophies" which might otherwise be viewed (at least in educational terms) as offering only tangential justifications for the subject. Thus, in the process of fighting for academic and professional status they had begun to incorporate aspects of ideologies beyond that of sport, such as health, PSE and even intellectual development.

It was noticeable, nonetheless, that views regarding the educational worth of PE were not expressed in the same manner as other ideological justifications. Indeed, they frequently appeared as afterthoughts — additional justifications in case enjoyment of sport was to be seen as insufficient in and of itself. It was as if teachers were claiming that sport is worthwhile for intrinsic reasons; however, if this was not considered a sufficient justification then a variety of additional "goods" might be used to bolster the position of PE.

PE Teachers' "Philosophies" as an Amalgam of Ideologies
It was apparent, then, that many PE teachers' "philosophies" incorporated several ideas or ideologies. Frequently these "philosophies" emphasised one dimension, typically sport, among an

amalgam featuring several additional aspects, such as health and "education for leisure" and "sport for all".

Change alongside Continuity

PE teachers' "philosophies" appeared to feature a characteristic of social development in general and the history of PE in the UK in particular: namely, the existence of continuity alongside change. Whilst real change may well have occurred in the ideologies and practices of PE teachers in the last 20 to 25 years (Evans, 1992; Kirk, 1992a), such change may not be as great or as transformative as one might want, or be inclined, to believe. Evidently, HRE has assumed a more prominent place in the "philosophies" and practices of PE teachers. At the same time, "education for leisure", together with "sport for all" and the promotion of active lifestyles, has become more central to PE teachers' views of what PE should be, and is, about. Nonetheless, it is apparent that widespread continuities persist alongside the occurrence of such real changes. Sport, and especially team games, remain at the heart of many teachers "philosophies" of PE (frequently alongside other justificatory ideologies) and continue to form the centrepiece of curricular and extra-curricular activities in secondary schools.

Based upon their research in the USA, Chen and Ennis (1996, p. 339) claimed that what they term the "discipline mastery" orientation (a "focus on developing performance proficiency in sport skills and understanding of performance-related knowledge") — what here is labelled the sporting ideology — "was no longer the dominant philosophy in teaching physical education". "Teachers' beliefs", they argued, "varied across the spectrum of the value orientations". My own study would not support such a claim. PE teachers' continuing and strong commitment to sport is a feature of their developing "philosophies". Whilst this may be tempered or even camouflaged by other concerns, such as concern for health and lifelong participation, most of them continue to view sport rather than physical activity as the most suitable and likely vehicle for achieving other "educational" goals.

Indeed, as Chen and Ennis (1996) acknowledge, even where PE teachers have value orientations other than sports performance — for example, what they refer to as "social responsibility" — they may well be constrained by subject-centred content in the curriculum.

This contextual constraint is precisely the situation that confronts PE teachers in England and Wales, faced with an activity-based NCPE that prioritises sport and, in particular, team games. In this regard, Penney and Evans (1999) have noted the constraints on the flexibility of teachers in England and Wales to achieve any kind of "slippage", as they put it, between the requirements of the sport and games privileged within NCPE and their own practice. Notwithstanding the discontinuing (in Curriculum 2000) of the requirement for older pupils to do games, it is evident that the Government has competitive sport in schools — and particularly in PE — high on its agenda ("Brooking talks on sport", 1999; Davies, 1999; Sport England, 2001) and that this will continue to act as a significant constraint upon teachers in practice. This would appear to cast doubt upon the extent to which, as Mawer (1996) suggests, teachers of PE do in practice have "philosophical" room for manoeuvre, whether or not they would be inclined to use it.

Philosophy and "Philosophies"
It was apparent that PE teachers tended not to have anything that could justifiably be called a "philosophy" as such — in the sense of an integrated, coherent set of ideas. Confusion and/or contradiction frequently characterised their commentaries. What PE teachers articulated was typically a kind of checklist of preferences revolving around words and phrases like "enjoyment", "health", "skills" and "sport for all". What they exhibited were commitments to particular ideologies, such as health promotion and sports performance and, frequently, a medley of ideologies to suit particular practical situations.

If one were to be kind one might describe these views in terms of what Reid (1997) refers to as "value pluralism" — a multiplicity of justifications for PE based on a plurality of values such as health, sports performance and character development. However, in reality, PE teachers' views were a pastiche of differing "philosophies" or, rather, ideologies (for example, regarding participation in lessons, health, personal and social education, school teams, sports performance and sporting skills) that were not always, or at least easily, reconcilable. Rather than representing a plurality of values, PE teachers seized upon things for justification; that is to say, they sought *ex post facto* justifications for the things they did and the things they preferred or felt constrained to do. In this regard, it was particularly interesting to note that in response to a follow-up question regarding why the things they had mentioned (such as enjoyment, health and sport) were important, many teachers appeared somewhat surprised by the question, as if they had never really given the matter much thought or that the question was redundant because the answer was self-evident.

It seems inappropriate, therefore, to label PE teachers' thoughts (about the nature and purposes of PE) "philosophies" as such — in anything other than the aphoristic, everyday sense indicated by placing quotation marks around the term. The "philosophies" articulated by the teachers referred to in this book gave the impression of "standing back" (or being detached) only marginally from either their preconceptions regarding the nature and intrinsic worth of PE and sport or the everyday "ephemeral urgencies" of being a PE teacher. At the same time, their "philosophies" frequently lacked any indication of an "overview" as such. Indeed, the views of teachers on particular dimensions of their "philosophies" (for example, participation levels and "sport for all") often stood in marked contrast to other dimensions (for example, standards of PE dress, school teams and performance sport).

It was interesting to note that the comments of many teachers in this study were of a piece with those of the PE teachers cited in Mason's (1995) study, who appeared to hold a similar "mish-mash" of views on PE. If this study, and that of Mason, are anything to go by, teachers' somewhat vague and unclear statements regarding the nature of PE suggest that they have little or no idea of philosophical conceptions of PE. Teachers' conceptions of PE bore only a passing resemblance to the variety of philosophical conceptions of the subject typical of academic analyses (see, for example, Arnold, 1997; Carr, 1997; Parry, 1998; Reid, 1996a, 1996b, 1997, 1999). Consequently, PE teachers' "philosophies" did not — nor could "philosophies" of the aphoristic kind be reasonably expected to — bear other than superficial resemblance to the putative abstract, systematic outlines of a set of coherent principles regarding the alleged nature and purposes of PE, of the type one might expect from an academic philosophical perspective.

The "philosophies" of PE teachers are not, then, philosophical as such. Rather, they are, more usually, an amalgam of beliefs, values and attitudes — of ideologies — that emerge from a figuration of the teachers' personal and sporting biographies and their working context. What Reid (1999, p. 103) refers to as "metatheoretical uncertainty" to describe the "plurality" of competing "philosophies" among PE teachers would — from a figurational sociological perspective — be better described as a fusion of prior values, beliefs and commitments more-or-less permeated and amended in accordance with experience and more-or-less adapted to fit the practical constraints of the day-to-day job of teaching.

The impact of philosophy as such on teachers' "philosophies", was, perhaps unsurprisingly from a sociological perspective, demonstrably very limited. What did impact upon PE teachers was their deeply rooted attachments and associated convictions (for example, towards the value of sport) and their practice — or, rather, the constraints circumscribing their practice. The way teachers thought about PE had been shaped by their past experiences and had become bound up with the job itself. As such, their "philosophies" tended to be *practical* "philosophies". Accordingly, an abiding theme of this study has been the claim that in order to make sense of PE teachers' "philosophies" one must recognise that people can only be understood — or, to couch the point in Eliasian terms, PE teachers only emerge as people — when their views are seen in the context of their time and related to the framework of their period (Elias, 1993). In this vein, teachers' thoughts on PE need to be viewed as aspects of their networks of social relationships, past and present. We need to appreciate the manner in which PE teachers' work is circumscribed by wider social processes (such as the medicalisation of life and the professionalisation of work). As Elias notes:

> individual decisions remain ultimately opaque if we overlook the relevant aspects of the unplanned social processes within which they are taken. (Elias, 1993, p. 46)

Whether they realise it or not, whether they like it or not, PE teachers are caught up in unplanned social processes, such as the medicalisation of life. More directly, they are heavily immersed in wider professional processes, such as the academicisation of (nominally) practical subjects such as PE. The upshot of these processes is that PE teachers frequently feel themselves compelled to do things — such as develop HRE and examinations in PE — and have to find some way (frequently retrospectively) to justify their actions. It is evident, then, that PE teachers compromise. They feel that they have to (or at least feel under great pressure to), not (or, at least, not entirely) because they are ideologues but, in part, because of the constraints with which they are faced. They may not have to believe in or perform certain practices (in a deterministic sense), but they feel as if they do; or, rather, they feel as if they have little choice or room for manoeuvre. What might be construed as an ideological conservatism on the part of teachers is only part of the story, so to speak. It is, also, a conservatism at a much more practical level: people tend not to want disruption or hostility to the routine working life that they have spent so much time and energy becoming accustomed to and, consequently, socialised into. This is not to say, however, that PE teachers' thoughts and practices are simply a reflection of their circumstances. There was ample evidence of teachers working behind the scenes to put into practice their preferred view of PE. But these, themselves, were frequently views or "philosophies" constrained by experience (for example, a negative impression of PE gained in childhood or the difficulties of maintaining interest among their protégés as a teacher).

This is a point worth dwelling upon: teachers perceived greater or lesser degrees of freedom and constraint in their circumstances whilst at the same time holding stronger or weaker views on PE per se. Thus, in the final part of this concluding chapter, I want to summarise how the "philosophies" held by PE teachers and their underlying ideologies can best be explained in terms of the networks of social relationships — or figurations — of which they are a part.

PE Teachers in their Figurations

It is with PE teachers that the various ideologies within the subject-community find expression. In attempting to understand PE teachers "philosophies", and the ideologies that underpin them, it is necessary to make sense of the figurations that teachers form with others. This, in turn, requires an awareness of the social characteristics of PE teachers themselves, in addition to an appreciation of the nature of teachers' interdependent relationships with others, at what I am calling the local and national levels of their figurations.

PE Teachers' Figurations at the Personal Level

Van Krieken defines the concept of *habitus* as:

> the durable and generalized disposition that suffuses a person's action throughout an entire domain of life or, in the extreme instance, throughout all of life—in which case the term comes to mean the whole manner, turn, cast, or mold of the personality. (Camic, 1986; cited in van Krieken, 1998, p. 47)

He elaborates on the usefulness of the concept by outlining the claim that the ideas one expresses — which come to the surface, so to speak—are by no means necessarily the ones that have most influence on our conduct. These, it is argued, are the "superficial" aspects of our consciousness whilst "the real forces which govern us" (Camic, 1986; cited in van Krieken, 1998, p. 47) are habits or habitus. It behoves the sociologist, then, to identify "the web of social relations in which the individual lives during his [*sic*] more impressionable phase, during childhood and youth" in the expectation that it will be these that have become imprinted "upon the unfolding personality" (Elias, 1994; cited in van Krieken, 1998, p. 156). In this regard, it is evident that PE teachers' commitment to sport and physical activity in one domain of their lives (their leisure) suffuses another domain (their working lives). Their biographies, and particularly their early and profound attachments to sport, appear to have developed a typical orientation towards PE among many teachers—that is to say, both in terms of what they think PE should be about as well as what they claim to do in practice. Teachers' biographies lent weight to a conceptualisation of childhood and youth as "the main 'transmission belt' for the development of habitus" (van Krieken, 1998, p. 156) — habituses that have come to characterise social groups such as PE teachers.

For Elias, because "habitus and culture are very slow to change" (van Krieken, 1998, p. 49) it becomes "impossible to understand social life except over longer spans of time" (p. 154). Such longer spans of time would, of course, involve more than the life spans of individual teachers or, for that matter, the relatively young history of PE in schools. Nonetheless, the notion of emergent and developing habituses helps one appreciate the fact that PE teachers do not arrive for teacher training as *tabulae rasae*. Rather, they arrive with particular dispositions towards PE, which, among other things, incorporate a "second nature" tendency to view PE as primarily to do with sport. As these teachers move into the world of PE teaching—and their figurations expand and become more complex—their habituses inevitably become connected to their emerging social relations. Thus, it is at the local and national levels of these figurations—when dispositions become configured with the contexts of particular social circumstances, such as the working environment—that PE teachers' intuitive orientations towards PE can be more-or-less challenged or reinforced. In practice, they seem, more often than not, to be reinforced. In this regard, it was interesting to note that, even though some teachers in my study suggested they had begun their PE teaching careers with a particular "philosophy", they claimed to have developed other interests (for example, health-related PE) over time that had influenced their practice, and subsequently their "philosophies"—for these, too, required *ex post facto* justification.

From a figurational perspective, it is crucial to appreciate that the figurations of which individuals are a part have immense significance for their nascent identities. And, because "personal and collective identities" are particularly important in the world of sport (Dunning, 1996, p. 188), PE teachers' networks can be said to be of particular significance for a sociological attempt to construct an adequate explanation of their "philosophies". PE teachers' thoughts, as well as their proffered practices, are characterised by degrees of involvement and detachment, not least in terms of the ties that bind them to particular we-groups—ranging from school PE departments (at the professional level) to particular sporting communities. As a result, teachers are more-or-less susceptible to what Elias (1993) terms the compulsion of the figuration. In this context, it is something of a truism for figurational sociologists that "People model their ideas about all their experiences chiefly on their experiences within their own groups" (Elias, 1978, p. 55).

PE Teachers' Figurations at the Local Level

PE teachers arrive at school with generalised dispositions towards PE. They have particular ideas regarding what they expect to be doing. To the extent that would-be teachers feel bound to incorporate particular views and practices in order to qualify as teachers, those "philosophies" are, in part, infused with the norms of their training. Typically, however, they owe a good deal more to their prior socialisation—that is to say, the habits or habitus acquired throughout their young lives.

As teachers, they find themselves enmeshed within a variety of practices, constraints and expectations, and the socialisation process continues. These constraints are many and varied. In brief, they include the constraints posed by significant others (such as head teachers, HoDs as well as more established PE colleagues, the pupils themselves and their parents), local constraints such as the inheritance of traditions (in a variety of forms, ranging from the more direct influence of sporting traditions through to the more indirect traditions such as the religious affiliation of schools), and what might be termed relatively self-imposed constraints (in the form of other roles they or their colleagues may have within the school but also beyond it), as well as self-imposed constraints that reflect issues at the national level of teachers' figurations (such as the development of examinations in PE as a response to collective status concerns).

Thus, it is argued, "philosophies" tend to be more influenced by practices, rather than preceded by them, and PE teachers' views become more comprehensible when viewed, at least in part, as responses to their day-to-day situations. Making sense of the way PE teachers think about their work requires one to think less about philosophies per se and more about the deep-seated values, beliefs and attitudes that they bring to their work. It also requires one to think more about the manner in which the context of this work constrains their practice — and, ultimately, their thoughts. In order to do this, one needs to locate the way in which PE teachers think about their work within the broader and day-to-day constraints of their work and their lives.

PE Teachers' Figurations at the National Level

In this book, I have attempted to show how the personal and local dimensions of PE teachers' figurations relate to developments at the national level. I have argued that developments such as NCPE, which have their origins at the national level, serve to constrain teachers at the local level of the school and inevitably come up against the group and individual habituses of PE teachers. These frequently coincide, giving the impression of a group habitus in the sense of a shared fund of common-sense understandings among particular groups of PE teachers.

The emerging public and political concerns with, for example, youth culture, the health of the nation and national sporting performance, which have characterised public policy from the 1960s onwards, render more complex and more opaque the figurations of which PE teachers were, and are, a part. In this vein, the significance of developments at the national level—for PE teachers' "philosophies", their underlying ideologies and their practice—waxes and wanes to the extent that the views of Government, various lobbies, the general public and the PE subject-community, as well as other interested parties, more-or-less coincide.

Developments in the socio-political milieu of PE inevitably enable or constrain some teachers more than others. Many teachers come to PE teaching, as a career, with a built-in commitment to sport and an intuitive conviction regarding its inherent worth. Inevitably, in terms of what they actually do as teachers, they are constrained by their circumstances—not simply the practical circumstances of managing the pupils but also the ideological circumstances manifest, for example, in what teachers inherit as a curriculum, the expectations of their managers, government legislation (for example, NCPE) and policy (for example, DCMS, 2000; DNH, 1995), and wider social and professional processes (such as the medicalisation of life and academicisation and professionalisation of PE), to name but a few of the more salient features.

Figurations and Power-Ratios at the Local and National Levels
Developments in the PE subject-community inevitably bear the hallmark of shifting balances of power within but also across a variety of PE and non-PE communities and groups. Thus, an underlying theme in the exploration of the significance of networks of interdependency for PE teachers' "philosophies" is a central dimension of figurations: namely, that of power. Whilst interdependencies are "reciprocal" they are also, and at whatever level they are to be found, typically unequal: "usually one party in a social relationship tends, at least in certain respects, to be more dependent than the other party", with the result that an uneven balance of power—or "power-ratio"—exists that "directly affects

the way both parties act and feel towards each other" (Mennell and Goudsblom, 1998, p. 22).

Whatever the particular nuances of each teacher's situation, PE teachers — as workers — live their working lives in social relationships and feel the effects of these, particularly the *power* effects. Moreover, these are not limited to the effects of face-to-face relationships with their immediate colleagues. Although the immediate working relationships (for example, within departments) have considerable effect upon their lives, PE teachers are also bound in to wider relational networks involving power-ratios that they might not readily recognise. For example, whether they like it or not, PE teachers are bound in to relations with the Government through government agencies, such as OFSTED and Sport England, and through legislation, such as NCPE. In addition, they are interdependent with what might be termed the "sports lobby" (governing bodies of sport, sports clubs and so on), teaching colleagues and professional bodies, not to mention the children they teach and their parents. These groups can, and do, affect the lives of PE teachers — their autonomy, their "philosophies", their job satisfaction and even their careers. Relations of power between individuals and groups develop as shifts and transformations in patterns of social bonding take place (Murphy *et al.*, 2000), and these involve shifts and transformations in the influence of some over others. And it is not just groups in the present that affect teachers: group ideologies from the recent past (for example, "traditional games") continue to affect the expectations teachers have of themselves and that others — be they parents, children or government ministers — have of them.

In terms of the relationships between various groups in the PE policy-community (Houlihan, 1991), the concepts of established-outsider relations (Scotson and Elias, 1994) and power- and status-differentials (van Krieken, 1998) helps one understand PE teachers' apparent preoccupation with status concerns and the relationship between these and the emergence of professional ideologies "which operate with greater or lesser success to enhance the status of particular [groups]" (van Krieken, 1998, p. 139). Hence the evident concern amongst physical educationalists with, for example, health promotion through PE as a means of achieving greater power in relation to other professional groupings both within and without education. Similarly, exploring the interrelationships between the local and national dimensions of PE teachers' figurations encourages an appreciation of "the position of knowledge production within *power* relations" (van Krieken, 1998, p. 169; emphasis in the original). These relations have fluctuated in the last quarter of a century or so, first appearing to move towards the pre-eminence of a health-related ideology before shifting back in the direction of the more enduring ideology of sport.

PE Teachers in their Figurations

It is not surprising to find that the configuration of circumstances and relationships in which PE teachers find themselves enmeshed is not typically conducive to the development of a relatively detached perspective on PE of the kind that might be associated (justifiably or otherwise) with the abstract theorising of educational philosophers. In a nutshell, along with individual and group habitus, the context within which teachers operate tends to be far more influential than any "philosophical" stance towards which they might be more-or-less inclined. Indeed, not only will context be more influential upon teachers' practice than theoretical considerations, but context is also likely to lead teachers to amend, adapt or even alter their "philosophies" in line with the constraints of their practice. As Connell (cited in Sparkes, 1990, p. 39) pithily observes: "...teachers are workers, teaching is work, and the school is a workplace. These simple facts are often forgotten." PE teachers respond to the immediate pressures of their working situation as involved participants. Consequently, their practice is typically more *reactive* than *proactive*. Where there is "tension" between practice and "philosophy", it tends to be the latter that is modified.

Philosophical versus Sociological Conceptions of PE

A philosopher of PE wrote recently that:

> when occasional and unsystematic reflection...begins to acquire a more systematic character, when we try to organize our thinking in a logically coherent and structured way, consciously seeking greater rigour and depth in our deliberations, then we are engaged in what can fairly be called the theory of our professional practice. (Reid, 1999, p. 102)

Notwithstanding the accuracy of this claim, it has been an enduring theme of this book that, to the extent that PE teachers do engage in "theorising", this tends to be a long way short of the kind of philoso-phising that academics engage in. On the whole, it was evident that PE teachers' "knowledge", as manifest in their "philosophies" of PE, tended to take the form of beliefs, wishes and what might be termed "articles of faith" rather than the kind of abstract theorising of the kind associated with the academic or even professional PE litera-ture. Thus, PE teachers in this study proffered little that could be said to resemble closely the academic philosophies of PE — in conventional phraseology or otherwise — in circulation at the level of PE theorising. On the other hand, however, it is worthy of note that many offered views that might be seen as *approximating* to the valued cultural practices justification articulated by Hirst (1994) and Arnold (1997) and the conceptually similar philosophy of sport education of Siedentop (1994). However, such comments *were* only approximations, for responses tended to take the form of clichés and were characterised by an absence of reflection. Indeed, one might speculate that the greater similarity of the more "PE friendly" valued cultural practice philosophy — that Hirst (1994), for example, has come to prefer over the standard "PE *un*friendly" academic conception of education (and thus PE) — might tell us more about perceived needs and related pressures to find teleological justifi-cations for PE in pressing circumstances than any enlightened coming together of the philosophical analysis of PE with PE practice. Indeed, it might tell us more about the prevalence of enlightened self-interest as a dynamic in PE.

Reid, like Carr (1997) before him, claims that:

> occasional detachment for the purposes of reflection…can hardly be regarded as an idle distraction from more urgent business; it has to be seen, rather, as an indispensable obligation for any properly consci-entious professional. (Reid, 1999, pp. 101-102)

Once again, however, we are confronted here with the limitations of a philosophical approach to making sense of knowledge in general, and the "philosophies" of PE teachers in particular. Philosophising about PE — at least in the academic sense — involves the develop-ment of systems of ideas with such a high degree of internal coher-ence and consistency and abstraction that they might be said to "stand alone", as it were. However, as this study has illustrated, as far as PE teachers are concerned, this is precisely what abstract academic philosophical conceptions of PE, in fact, do: they stand alone, almost entirely ignored by PE teachers. Putting to one side the question of whether "any properly conscientious professional" is, indeed, "*obliged*" (emphasis added) to philosophise, it is clear that PE teachers tend not do so or, at the very least, do so in a very tenuous form and very infrequently, if at all.

Reid (1999, p. 104) continues:

> For if there are conflicts or problems with the theoretical framework of ideas and presuppositions which governs our professional practice, then we must not be surprised if those conflicts or problems find a way of manifesting themselves at the level of our concrete practical activity.

From a sociological perspective, such a claim is highly debatable inasmuch as theoretical problems do not appear to manifest themselves in teachers' practice, or, at least, not to the extent that Reid implies. Nor, for that matter, do ideas "govern" professional practice; arguably, indeed, the reverse is more typically the case.

PE teachers are constrained in a way that philosophers of PE are not. Philosophers — in part, because it is part and parcel of their occupation — are *relatively* free (indeed, are obliged) to contemplate abstract ideas regarding the nature and purposes of PE, such as they are. As Elias (1993) might argue, academic philosophers of PE have tended to philosophise with the presumption of people not dependent upon the need to adapt their thoughts to the lived reality of teachers, for example, for their professional survival. It is worth remembering, however, that philosophers and academics are themselves constrained by the demands of being professional philosophers and academics. They are constrained in different ways to, and in different directions from, PE teachers; that is to say, the *structure* of their work is different from that of PE teachers. Nonetheless, their job provides sufficient leeway to enable them to indulge in preferred views. Philosophers themselves can, quite readily, become vehicles (some might say the primary vehicles) for ideologies — whether of sport (Siedentop, 1994), moral education (Laker, 1996a, 1996b) or "Olympism" (Parry, 1998). Arguably, then, the philosophies of philosophers share something in common with the everyday "philosophies" of PE teachers, inasmuch as they may be more adequately conceptualised as constituting *justificatory* ideologies (a point I will return to shortly). In this respect, philosophers' philosophising upon PE frequently appears quite involved, not to say evaluative. As such, their thoughts may tell us more about the ideological commitments of these philosophers than about any prescribed purposes for PE. Whilst giving the impression of not being so, the arguments of philosophers are frequently more-or-less ideological and are made relatively opaque by their ostensible claims to be discussing the nature and purposes of PE in an abstract, detached manner. In the process, they effectively obscure rather than clarify our understanding. As Mennell and Goudsblom (1998, p. 33) observe, "thanks to the power of philosophers as an established group within universities" in the UK, and the associated centrality of educational philosophy to PE since the late 1960s, the writings of authors in the philosophy of PE tradition have had a significant impact on *theoretical* justifications for PE in both the academic and teaching worlds (if not everyday "philosophies").

Indeed, it might be added that what McNamee (1998, p. 75) refers to as the "cognitive imperialism" of the "traditional liberal paradigm" of education (as initiation of young people into the forms of knowledge that constitute the "rational mind" and thus develop autonomous adults) has served to constrain the manner in which educationalists *at all levels* have felt able to articulate views on the nature and purposes of their subject. Here, then, in the "cognitive imperialism" of analytical philosophy, is one clear and immediate illustration of the penetration of social processes into the process of philosophising—at the level of PE teachers as well as academic philosophers.

Thus, the abstract philosophical contemplation of concepts such as education that has characterised the orthodox "analytical" philosophy of education can, when viewed sociologically, be seen to bear the hallmark of a greater degree of involvement than might be recognised or acknowledged by philosophers themselves. McNamee (1998, p.87) points out that "...to set out the traditional liberal distinctions" to be found in conceptions of education renders them "open to the simple charge of ideology; no matter how internally coherent the thesis", they "are always open to counter-ideological critique". It is necessary, McNamee adds, to recognise that a plurality of conceptions of PE (as well as education) is likely to exist depending upon the "shared understanding" (1998, p. 87) of particular groups. Thus, academic philosophers of all varieties, under the "pretext" of saying what PE is about are "really saying" what they think it "ideally should be" (Elias, 1978, p. 52). For Elias, philosophers and people in general, for that matter, have a tendency to "confuse fact with ideal, that which *is* with that which *ought* to be" (Elias, 1978, p. 118; emphases added).

The "distinctive role" of the philosophy of PE, according to Reid (1999, p. 103), might be said to be exploration of the question "How [do] we conceptualise or think about issues in physical education?" For a figurational sociologist, however, such an undertaking is a quintessentially *sociological* task. From a figurational perspective, what teachers think and why they think it — as well as what they actually do in practice — only becomes fully intelligible with reference to their habituses and contexts. This is the central point of this book: only an approach that incorporates sociology can adequately explain *why* teachers think *what* they think.

A Figurational Sociological Epistemology

The central argument of this book is, I hope, clear. PE teachers' "philosophies" (or even, for that matter, the views of professional academic philosophers) cannot readily be understood only, or even mainly, in terms of any apparently abstract reasoning on their part. In the same way that what PE teachers think cannot be understood in isolation from what they do, what they think cannot be understood without fully appreciating the significance of the emotional dimension to thinking and acting. It is here that the benefits of a sociological (and specifically, figurational) perspective on epistemological issues are apparent. As with agency theorists, the attachment of philosophers of the analytic school "to individualist liberal ideals of autonomy and freedom", as van Krieken (1998, p. 45) puts it, gets in the way of their attempts comprehensively and adequately to conceptualise knowledge. One cannot make any sense of knowledge or the process of thinking if one attempts to do so on the basis of a presumption of rationality alone, or even primarily. Reasoning, as a process, is an acquired ability — that is to say, one that is learned. Acquiring the propensity to reason, however crucial, is only one dimension of the process of thinking. The thinker also needs to be inclined towards applying reason in a sufficiently detached manner if reasoning is to serve the end of attaining object-adequate knowledge. Otherwise, the process of reasoning will inevitably be more-or-less affected by the magnetic "pull" of the emotions — of the thinker's *involvement*. The "attraction" of involvement is likely to undermine the adequacy of the thought process by pulling reasoning in the direction of the thinker's intuitive, preferred perspective on any given topic.

From a sociological standpoint, appreciation of the more-or-less ideological nature of conceptions of PE points towards Mannheim's (1960, p. 71) conclusion that "the vain hope of discovering truth in a form which is independent of an historically and socially determined set of meanings will have to be given up".

"Philosophies" of PE as Justificatory Ideologies of PE

It is claimed, then, that investigating PE teachers' perspectives in the context of the figurations of which they are a part proves far more informative in making sense of their "philosophies", ideologies and practice than what might be termed the "grand [academic] philosophies" circulating in the subject-community. Having noted the significance of contextual constraints, however, it is important to bear in mind that it remains an open question whether or not these constraints serve to hinder many (and especially male) teachers from pursuing their "ideal" PE provision. For it may be that such constraints provide a convenient fund of "handy" justifications for what, in reality, amount to many teachers' preferred practices: sport and team games. PE teachers are more-or-less predisposed towards particular ideologies. These ideologies, in configuration with the practical constraints they confront, manifest themselves in particular "philosophies" as well as practices. Such "philosophies" are better viewed, it is argued, as *justificatory ideologies*. Of course, aspects of PE teachers' "philosophies" may, to a greater or lesser extent, be related to factual knowledge of a broadly scientific, even philosophical, kind. More often, however, they tend to be an amalgam of values, beliefs and pragmatism and, thus, frequently share one thing in common: a tendency to rely on theoretical knowledge as a "prop" for a preferred way of seeing the world. Consequently, it is argued that much of the "knowledge" that constitutes PE teachers' "philosophies" is, in fact, ideological and, as such, is more-or-less mythical.

The distortions characteristic of ideological thinking among PE teachers in the present study appeared reminiscent of what Mannheim (1960, p. 49) would refer to as unwitting "self-deception". For the most part, these distortions are a consequence of the social situation teachers found themselves in contemporarily (in the form of their context) as well as over the course of their lives (in the form of their habitus). Such ideological thinking is, frequently, neither the result of deliberate attempts to deceive, at one pole, nor "error...[as] the result of a distorted and faulty conceptual apparatus, at the other" (Mannheim, 1960, p. 54). Teachers' ideologies are more adequately conceptualised as the product of the figurations of which they are a part — that is to say, the particular networks of relationships that serve to constrain and shape their "philosophies" and practices as they develop and, in the process, make commitment to some ideologies more likely than others.

In this book I have attempted to show how "philosophies" of PE teachers are embedded in a particular culture at a particular time. PE teachers' thoughts are constrained by their figurations and consequently culled from a common fund of everyday ideas. Thus, it is important to note that ideologies, as Dunning (1992, p. 187) says of theories in general, "become fashionable for a greater or lesser period of time for extra-scientific reasons" and frequently this leads to an "uncritical submission to the authority and prestige of the dominant standards" (Elias in Mennell and Goudsblom, 1998, p. 231). Mannheim (1960) draws our attention to the empirical tendency for ideologies to develop in conflict situations as a defence of or attack on something, and hence their propensity to distort. In this vein, Elias (in Mennell and Goudsblom, 1998, p. 227) points out that people:

> work and live in a world in which almost everywhere groups, small and great, including their own groups, are engaged in a struggle for position and often enough for survival, some trying to rise and better themselves in the teeth of strong opposition, some who have risen before trying to hold on to what they have, and some going down.

"Philosophies" were frequently justified "by drawing upon convenient and readily available rationale" (Waddington *et al.*, 1998, p. 42). Rationale based upon academic consideration, in particular, tended to lend degrees of respectability (Waddington *et al.*, 1998) to preferred views of PE. Indeed, the point made by Waddington *et al.*

regarding gender stereotypes among PE teachers can be generalised to their "philosophies" as a whole:

> the recourse of many teachers to pseudo-educational rationales to support...stereotypical views is perhaps indicative of the amount, and the strength, of resistance to change. (Waddington *et al.*, 1998, p. 44)

Given that diverse and multi-faceted societies contain a plurality of ideologies, it is unsurprising to find that education and PE contain a range of ideologies and vested interests within which some are more prominent than others. PE teachers' (both as individuals and as groups) "philosophies" tend to be characterised by a mixture of ideologies, with some (such as health but more especially sport) more prominent than others. However, the dynamic nature of the figurations of which PE teachers are a part means that relatively pre-eminent ideologies never completely subjugate others, not least because of the differentially powerful influences within the differing figurations (for example, of women PE teachers, those in deprived areas and so forth).

Given, also, the apparent significance of teachers' habituses and contexts for their views of PE, coupled with constraints on academics to engage, to a greater or lesser extent, in theoretical debate, perhaps one should not be surprised to find that the former have often been criticised in the academic and professional press for being uncritical and unreflective—for taking a somewhat "rosy" and conservative view of what PE "is about" and what it actually achieves. It has long appeared to be a widely held belief among physical educationalists that simply participating in sport would lead to the development of desirable personal and social benefits, and a number of authors have observed that the PE profession characteristically and routinely fails to reflect upon its rationale and practice. Evans and Davies (1986) have suggested that one reason why PE has largely been neglected as an area of the school curriculum is precisely because teachers of PE themselves have by and large failed to take a "reflexive attitude" towards their practices and the "rationales which sustain them". In this regard, Kirk (1992b, p. 225) points to what he perceives as an apparent ambivalence towards many issues on the part of physical educationalists and believes that "it suggests an absence of critical awareness of social and cultural phenomena which are of direct relevance to the work [physical educationalists] do". And yet, it is worth observing that, from a sociological perspective, this should not be at all surprising if one recognises, to put it starkly, that PE is *not* full of philosophers! Evans and Davies's (1986, p. 16) comment that conservatism "sometimes appears as inherent in the Physical Education profession" should not surprise us either. The PE profession is not unique here — this is a normal characteristic of occupational groups who have a built-in tendency to resist change that threatens to make life highly uncomfortable by disrupting established routines.

Alderson and Crutchley (1990) offer a more detailed attempt to explain this perceived state of affairs and suggest that it may be explainable in terms of the following factors: the lack of a constructively critical perspective within teacher training (and hence within teaching itself); the lack of an evaluative perspective and the discouragement of those who have doubts about or wish to question accepted practice; a preoccupation with sporting competition and the development of talent; a suspicion that training institutions have recruited to the profession many people who are keenly interested in high-level sport but who are less interested in teaching or the less-able pupil; the fact that teachers have neither the time nor the skills to plan and evaluate their own work effectively enough; and, finally, fragmentation within the profession and a lack of unity amongst the various representative organisations.

Despite the intuitive plausibility of such an explanation, from a sociological perspective, Alderson and Crutchley appear to have confused what might, at the risk of over-simplification, be referred to as "cause and effect". PE teachers tend to have certain predispositions — certain habituses — and are surrounded by a variety of more-or-less common constraints. It is perfectly understandable, then, that there exists a lack of critical reflective thinking on the part of PE teachers about what they do. The point is that it is somewhat misguided to place undue emphasis upon the role of PE philosophy or, for that matter, PE teachers' "philosophies" in the aphoristic sense, as a major determinant of PE teachers' behaviour. It remains an open question, as van Krieken (1998) might put it, whether or not the group habitus of PE teachers has changed (for example, in the direction of concern for health promotion as the primary rationale of PE) to the extent that some (for example, Murdoch, 1992) might want to think it has; for, as van Krieken (1998, p. 70) notes, "it is largely part of the modern self-perception to want to see ourselves as radically different from our historical predecessors", not least, one might add, in the hope that a distancing from "playing" sport to promoting health might lend academic and professional credence to the various groups in the PE subject-community.

The changing formations that characterise habitus are not yet as pronounced in the world of the PE teacher as some might suppose. The "continual adjustment of human conduct and action to particular social conditions" (van Krieken, 1998, p. 174) appears manifest in several developments that PE teachers seem to have been relatively keen to support, such as HRE and examinable PE. Hence, the emergence of various medium- or long-term shifts in ideological pre-eminence, which tell us something about "the balance between continuity and change" (Dunning, 1996, p. 186) in ideological trends in PE.

In sociological terms, it is important to recognise that the case of PE may be one more example of a tendency to treat as purposive what is, in fact, by and large unplanned: a consequence of the "to-ing and fro-ing" of the power-ratios within and without PE. Whilst not planned, nor indeed intended, many developments in PE (such as the continuing pre-eminence of team games and sport in curricular and extra-curricular PE) have not been unstructured nor have they been random. Although not deliberately developed in a particular direction, trends in ideological influence have developed a recognisable pattern: one that reflects both the ideological inclinations of a large number of (especially male) PE teachers and a variety of influential groups in the PE policy-community. Teachers' "philosophies" of extra-curricular PE in particular — as well as their professed practice — tell us one very important thing: namely, that when they can, when given a relatively free hand, many PE teachers (female as well as male) are inclined to choose sport. When the constraints of NCPE, classroom management and such like are diminished, many PE teachers tend to fall back on their own commitments and values — they fall back upon sport. Such tendencies act as a kind of self-constraint of teachers upon themselves. They are, in turn, exacerbated by wider social processes, such as the emergence of a quasi-market in education and official and semi-official publications that have served to renew emphasis upon sport and, in particular, team games. At the same time, however, to the extent that concerns internal to the profession (for example, status) configure with wider social developments and processes (health concerns), traditionally pre-eminent ideologies (such as sport) have not gone unchallenged or, for that matter, unmodified.

The "fundamental changes in educational philosophies and organisation" (Waddington *et al.*, 1998, p. 34) have been mirrored, at least in part, by the emergence of health-related and, to a lesser extent, "education for leisure" or "sport for all" justificatory ideologies for PE on the part of teachers. Nonetheless, there was substantial evidence to suggest that both male and female PE teachers' "philosophies" remain strongly wedded to the sporting ideology first and foremost. NCPE has tended to reinforce the existing balance in favour of a sporting ideology.

Policy Implications and Current Developments

PE teachers are, as it were, at the "sharp end" of PE; it is the teachers who perform the practice of PE. If we wish to understand teachers' "philosophies" of PE, then we must study them not as abstract philosophical systems of ideas, but rather as practical, everyday "philosophies" that provide practical guides to action as well as a justification for those actions. It becomes particularly important to appreciate the policy implications of such a realisation in relation to recent developments. In this final section, therefore, I want to consider briefly the policy implications of this study for two groups of people who in one way or another attempt to influence PE teachers' views of their subject as well as their practice: teacher-trainers and academics. In light of recent developments in relation to NCPE and government policy statements, it may be worthwhile drawing out the implications for government officials as well.

An example of the policy problems associated with a failure to grasp the lessons learned from a study such as this has come recently in several pronouncements from the chair of Sport England (and ex-professional footballer), Trevor Brooking, and successive Ministers for Sport. Brooking is regularly quoted (see, for example, "Brooking talks on sport", 1999) as suggesting that curricular and extra-curricular PE are in need of an overhaul. He claims that the "skills [of pupils] have slid dramatically, compared to when he was at school, as a result of not enough competitive sport and not enough practice out of school hours" (p. 2). Brooking went on to say, "What we've got to do is try and *put a fun and enjoyment factor into sport and teach technical skills* without the pressure of success at all costs" (emphasis added). It is evident that the chair of Sport England and PE teachers are, indeed, "talking past one another", insofar as the former is clearly unaware that *enjoyment* of *sport* is one aspect of PE teachers' "philosophies" and practice that he need not be concerned about!

Around the time of Brooking's statement, the Minister for Sport commented that the proposals for the 2000 revision of NCPE aimed "to increase flexibility and promote participation by providing a wider choice of exercise options for pupils to select from" (cited in Davies, 1999, p. 40). Curriculum 2000 has made the activity area of games at Key Stage 4 an option rather than a requirement. Such an aim would be "in tune" with many teachers' ostensible desire for greater "activity choice", among older pupils especially. Nevertheless, this is an aim that appears somewhat "out of tune" with the policies of OFSTED as well as later declarations by the Minister herself, who goes on to acknowledge that "'bridging' will need to take place between the two Government departments" (Davies, 1999, p. 40) (that is to say, those of DfEE and DCMS) insofar as she "wants to make sure that no school will use it as an excuse for not having team sport" (p. 40). The data in this study suggests that, as far as PE teachers' are concerned, "activity choice" and sport are not mutually exclusive. PE teachers have a deep attachment to both. It is apparent that whilst PE teachers, academics and teacher-trainers appear keen to establish their academic credentials and thus their professional status, this does not seem to be the role that Government and the Sports Council have in mind for PE.

Successive Ministers for Sport's commitment to "changing the ethos of school sport, and *involving parents more*" (Davies, 1999, p. 40; emphasis added) suggests that the constraints operating at the national and local level of PE teachers' figurations will constrain them towards a sporting ideology. Insofar as such an ideology is more-or-less prominent in the "philosophies" of many teachers, recent developments appear unlikely to redress the balance of influence within PE that is tilted heavily towards sport rather than "education for leisure" / "sport for all" or even, for that matter, the ideology of health. It remains to be seen whether national con-

straints will impact significantly upon the process of academicisation in PE.

If the realities of PE teachers' figurations at the personal, local and
national levels are, as is claimed, of far greater significance (in terms
of their views of what they are trying to achieve) than the pros-
elytising of PE academics or even the policies of Government, it
seems evident that, to the extent to which academics in general, and
philosophers in particular, fail to engage with a sociological perspective on knowledge in PE, they fail to engage with the realities of
PE, rather than the mythology of PE. The message for those "wise"
people — academics and teacher-trainers as well as government
officials — who endeavour to establish influence over the development of the PE curriculum and, for that matter, PE teachers, is that
unless they take account of the realities of the people who implement curricula they will be unlikely to achieve their goals.

Whilst sociologists cannot say what PE teachers *ought* to be doing,
they can analyse and seek to understand why they *do* what they do
and why they *think* what they think. At the same time, sociologists
are in a position to throw light upon the prominent ideologies
within the subject-community and beyond and the relationship
between these and the "philosophies" (in the aphoristic sense) held
by PE teachers. As indicated at the outset of this book, this is
important for several reasons. Firstly, the absence of such an understanding will inevitably mean that PE teachers, teacher-trainers and
academics will be likely to misunderstand and "talk past one
another". Secondly, the share of resources devoted to particular
conceptions of PE and particular aims for PE will reflect the degree
of power maintained by particular groups favouring particular
conceptions. All philosophising and policy-making, it is argued,
need to be sociologically informed if they are to be concerned with
realistic aims in PE.

References

Alderson, J., & Crutchley, D. (1990). Physical education in the national curriculum. In N. Armstrong (Ed.), *New directions in physical education volume one* (pp. 37-62). Champaign, IL: Human Kinetics.

Alexander, K., Taggart, A., & Thorpe, S. (1996). A spring in their steps? Possibilities for professional renewal through sports education in Australian schools. *Sport, Education and Society, 1*(1), 23-46.

Almond, L. (1983). A rationale for health-related fitness. *The Bulletin of Physical Education, 19*(2), 5-10.

Almond, L. (1989). *The place of physical education in schools.* London: Kogan Page.

Almond, L. (1996). A new vision for physical education. In N. Armstrong (Ed.), *New Directions in Physical Education: Change and Innovation* (pp. 189-198). London: Cassell Education.

Almond, L., Harrison, P., & Laws, C. (1996). Sport: Raising the game—a physical education perspective. *The British Journal of Physical Education, 27*(3), 6-11.

American Alliance for Health, Physical Education, Recreation and Dance, The (AAHPERD) (1980). *Health related physical fitness test manual.* Reston, VA: AAHPERD.

Armour, K. (1997). Developing a personal philosophy on the nature and purpose of physical education: Life history reflections of physical education teachers at Citylimits high school. *European Physical Education Review, 3*(1), 68-82.

Armour, K., & Jones, R. (1998). *Physical education teachers' lives and careers: PE, sport and educational status.* Basingstoke: The Falmer Press.

Armstrong, N. (1987). Why implement a health-related fitness programme? *British Journal of Physical Education, 15*(6), 173-175.

Armstrong, N. (1990). Children's physical activity patterns: The implications for physical education. In N. Armstrong (Ed.), *New directions in physical education volume one* (pp. 1-16). Champaign, IL: Human Kinetics.

Armstrong, N., & Welsman, J. (1997). *Young people and physical activity.* Oxford: Oxford University Press.

Armstrong, N., McManus, A., Welsman, J., & Kirby, B. (1996). Physical activity patterns and aerobic fitness among prepubescents. *European Physical Education Review, 2*(1), 19-29.

Armstrong, N., Welsman, J., & Kirby, B. (1998). Aerobic fitness and physical activity patterns of young people. In K. Green & K. Hardman (Eds.), *Physical education: A reader* (pp. 105-115). Aachen: Meyer & Meyer Verlag.

Arnold, P. J. (1991). Health promotion in society, education and the movement curriculum. *Physical Education Review, 14*(2), 104-118.

Arnold, P. J. (1992). Sport as a valued human practice: A basis for the consideration of some moral issues in sport. *Journal of Philosophy of Education, 26*(2), 237-255.

References

Arnold, P. J. (1997). *Sport, ethics and education.* London: Cassell.

Biddle, S. (1987). *Foundations of health related fitness.* London: Ling Publishing.

Blake, B. (1996). Spiritual, moral, social and cultural development in physical education. *Bulletin of Physical Education, 32*(1), 6-16.

Bowling, A. (1997). *Research methods in health.* Buckingham: Open University Press.

Bray, S. (1991). Health-related physical activity in the primary school. In N. Armstrong & A. Sparkes (Eds.), *Issues in physical education* (pp. 170-189). Champaign, IL: Human Kinetics.

Brooker, R., Kirk, D., Braiuka, S., & Bransgrove, A. (2000). Implementing a game-sense approach to teaching junior high school basketball in a naturalistic setting. *European Physical Education Review, 6*(1), 7-26.

Brooking talks on sport. (1999). *Leisure Opportunities, 242,* 2.

Brown, D. (1999). Complicity and reproduction in teaching physical education. *Sport, Education and Society, 4*(2), 143-159.

Cale, L. (2000). Physical activity promotion in secondary schools. *European Physical Education Review, 6*(1), 71-90.

Carr, D. (1979). Aims of physical education. *Physical Education Review, 2*(2), 91-100.

Carr, D. (1997). Physical education and value diversity: A response to Andrew Reid. *European Physical Education Review, 3*(2), 95-105.

Carroll, B. (1994). *Assessment in physical education: A teachers guide to the issues.* London: The Falmer Press.

Carroll, B. (1998). The emergence and growth of examinations in physical education. In K. Green & K. Hardman (Eds.), *Physical education: A reader* (pp. 335-352). Aachen: Meyer & Meyer Verlag.

Carvel, J. (1999, 21 June). £60m sport fund to fire pupils will to win. *The Guardian,* p. 9.

Central Council for Physical Recreation (CCPR) (1960). *Sport and the community.* London: CCPR.

Chambers English dictionary. (1990). Edinburgh: W. & R. Chambers.

Chen, A., & Ennis, C. D. (1996). Teaching value-laden curricula in physical education. *Journal of Teaching in Physical Education, 15,* 338-354.

Colquhoun, D. (1991). Health based physical education: The ideology of healthism and victim blaming. *Physical Education Review, 14*(1), 5-13.

Colquhoun, D. (1992). Technocratic rationality and the medicalisation of the physical education curriculum. *Physical Education Review, 15*(1), 5-12.

Colquhoun, D., & Kirk, D. (1987). Investigating the problematic relationship between health and physical education: An Australian study. *Physical Education Review,10*(2), 100-109.

Colwell, S. (1999). Feminisms and figurational sociology: Contributions to understandings of sports, physical education and sex/gender. *European Physical Education Review, 5*(3), 241-262.

Corbin, D. E., Metal-Corbin, J., & Biddle, S. (1989). Educating children about ageing and lifetime health-related fitness. *The British Journal of Physical Education, 20*(4), 191-192.

Curtner-Smith, M. D. (1995). The more things change, the more they stay the same: Factors influencing teachers' interpretations and delivery of the National Curriculum Physical Education. *Sport, Education and Society, 4*(1), 75-97.

Curtner-Smith, M. D. (2001). The occupational socialization of a first-year physical education teacher with a teaching orientation. *Sport, Education and Sociey, 6*(1), 81-105.

Curtner-Smith, M. D., & Meek, G. (2000). Teachers' value-orientations and their compatibility with the National Curriculum for Physical Education. *European Physical Education Review, 6*(1), 27-45.

Davies, G.A. (1999, 17 September). Hoey has strategy to return team games to the agenda. *The Daily Telegraph,* p. 40.

Denscombe, M. (1998). *The good research guide.* Buckingham: Open University Press.

Department for Culture, Media and Sport (DCMS) (2000). *A sporting future for all: The government's plan for sport.* London: DCMS.

Department of Education and Science/Welsh Office (DES/WO) (1991). *Physical education for ages 5-16: Proposals of the Secretary of State for Education and the Secretary of State for Wales.* London: DES/WO.

Department of National Heritage (DNH) (1995). *Sport: Raising the game.* London: DNH.

Department of National Heritage (DNH) (1996). *Sport: Raising the game. One year on.* London: DNH.

Dewar, A. M., & Lawson, H. A. (1984). The subjective warrant and recruitment into physical education. *QUEST, 30,* 15-25.

Dunning E. (1992). Figurational sociology and the sociology of sport. In Centre for Research into Sport and Society (CRSS), *Theories of sport* (Module 2, Unit 3, pp. 147-221). Leicester: CRSS.

Dunning, E. (1996). On problems of the emotions in sport and leisure: Critical and counter-critical comments on the conventional and figurational sociologies of sport and leisure. *Leisure Studies, 15*(3), 185-207.

Dunning, E. (1999). *Sport matters.* London: Routledge.

Elias, N. (1978). *What is sociology?* London: Hutchinson.

Elias, N. (1993). *Mozart: Portrait of a genius.* Cambridge: Polity Press.

Evans, J. (1990). Defining a subject: The rise and rise of the new PE? *British Journal of Sociology of Education, 11*(2), 155-169.

Evans, J. (1992). A short paper about people, power and educational reform. Authority and representation in ethnographic research. Subjectivity, ideology and educational reform: The case of physical education. In A. C. Sparkes (Ed.), *Research in physical education and sport* (pp. 231-247). London: The Falmer Press.

Evans, J., & Davies, B. (1986). Sociology, schooling and physical education. In J. Evans (Ed.), *Physical education, sport and schooling: Studies in the sociology of physical education* (pp. 11-17). London: The Falmer Press.

Evans, J., Davies, B., & Penney, D. (1996). Teachers, teaching and the social construction of gender. *Sport, Education and Society, 1*(2), 165-184.

Evans, J., & Williams, T. (1989). Moving up and getting out: The classed and gendered opportunities of physical education teachers. In T. Templin & P. Schempp (Eds.), *Socialization into physical education: Learning to teach* (pp. 235-251).Indianapolis: Benchmark Press.

Fairclough, S., Stratton, G., & Baldwin, G. (2002). The contribution of secondary school physical education to lifetime physical activity. *European Physical Education Review, 8*(1), 69-84.

Fejgin, N. (1995). The academicization of physical education teacher training: A discourse analysis case study. *International Review for the Sociology of Sport, 30*(2), 179-190.

Fisher, R. (1996). Gifted children and young people in physical education and sport. In N. Armstrong (Ed.), *New directions in physical education: Change and innovation* (pp. 131-143). London: Cassell Education.

Flew, A. (1984). Preface. In A. Flew (Ed.), *A dictionary of philosophy* (2nd ed., pp. viixi). London: Pan Books.

Fox, K. R. (1983a). Physical lifeskills: Further thoughts on health-related fitness. *The British Journal of Physical Education, 14*(3), 68.

Fox, K. R. (1983b). Teaching physical lifeskills: Practical ideas on health-related fitness. *The British Journal of Physical Education, 14*(5), 126-128.

Fox, K. R. (1993). Exercise and the promotion of public health: More messages for the mission. *The British Journal of Physical Education, 24*(3), 36-39.

Fox, K. R. (1996). Physical activity promotion and the active school. In N. Armstrong (Ed.), *New directions in physical education: Change and innovation* (pp. 94-109). London: Cassell Education.

Frisby, D., & Sayer, D. (1986). *Society.* London: Ellis Horwood and Tavistock.

Giddens, A. (1984). *The constitution of society: Outline of the theory of structuration.* Cambridge: Polity Press.

Green, K. (1994). Meeting the challenge: Health-related exercise and the encouragement of lifelong participation. *The Bulletin of Physical Education, 30*(3), 27-34.

Green, K. (1998). Philosophies, ideologies and the practice of physical education. *Sport, Education and Society, 3*(2), 125-143.

Green, K. (2000). Exploring the everyday philosophies of physical education teachers from a sociological perspective. *Sport, Education and Society, 5*(2), 109-129.

Green, K. (2001). Examinations in physical education: A sociological perspective on a new orthodoxy. *British Journal of Sociology of Education, 22*(1), 51-73.

Green, K. (2002). Physical education, lifelong participation and the work of Ken Roberts. *Sport, Education and Society, 7* (2), 167-182.

Green, K., & Thurston, M. (2002). Physical education and health promotion: A qualitative study of teachers' perceptions. *Health Education, 102*(3), 113-123.

Hardman, K. (1998). To be or not to be? The present and future of school physical education in international context. In K. Green & K. Hardman (Eds.), *Physical Education: A reader* (pp. 353-382). Aachen: Meyer & Meyer Verlag.

Hargreaves, J. (1994). *Sporting females: Critical issues in the history and sociology of women's sports.* London: Routledge.

Harris, J. (1994a). Health-related exercise in the National Curriculum: Results of a pilot study in secondary schools. *The British Journal of Physical Education Research Supplement, 14,* 6-11.

Harris, J. (1994b). Young people's perceptions of health, fitness and exercise: Implications for the teaching of health related exercise. *Physical Education Review, 17*(2), 143-151.

Harris, J., & Cale, L. (1997). Activity promotion in physical education. *European Physical Education Review, 3*(1), 58-67.

Hendry, L. B. (1986). Changing schools in a changing society: The role of physical education. In J. Evans (Ed.), *Physical education, sport and schooling: Studies in the sociology of physical education* (pp. 41-70). Basingstoke: The Falmer Press.

Hendry, L. B., Shucksmith, J., Love, J. G., & Glendenning, A. (1993). *Young people's leisure and lifestyles.* London: Routledge.

Hirst, P. (1994, 9 July). From forms of knowledge to forms of practice. In *Working together for physical education.* The National Conference for Physical

Education, Sport and Dance, Loughborough University.

Holt, R. (1989). *Sport and the British: A modern history*. Oxford: Oxford University Press.

Houlihan, B. (1991). *The government and politics of sport*. London: Routledge.

Johns, D. J., Gilbert, K., & Shuttleworth, J. (1994). *Justifying terminology and changing discourses: From physical education to human movement studies*. Unpublished manuscript.

Kilminster, R. (1998). *The sociological revolution: From the Enlightenment to the global age*. London: Routledge.

Kirk, D. (1990). Defining the subject: Gymnastics and gender in British physical education. In D. Kirk & R. Tinning (Eds.), *Physical education, curriculum and culture: Critical issues in the contemporary crisis* (pp. 43-66). London: The Falmer Press.

Kirk, D. (1992a). *Defining physical education*. London: The Falmer Press.

Kirk, D. (1992b). Curriculum history in physical education: A source of struggle and a force for change. In A. C. Sparkes (Ed.), *Research in physical education and sport* (pp. 210-230). London: The Falmer Press.

Laker, A. (1996a). The aims of physical education within the revised National Curriculum: Lip service to the affective? *Pedagogy in Practice*, 2(1), 24-30.

Laker, A. (1996b). Learning to teach through the physical as well as of the physical. *The British Journal of Physical Education*, 27(3), 18-22.

Lawson, H. A. (1983a). Toward a model of teacher socialization in physical education: The subjective warrant, recruitment and teacher education. *Journal of Teaching in Physical Education*, 2, 3-16.

Lawson, H. A. (1983b). Toward a model of teacher socialization in physical education: Entry into schools, teachers role orientations, and longevity in teaching. *Journal of Teaching in Physical Education*, 3, 3-15.

Lawson, H. A. (1988). Occupational socialization, cultural studies and the physical education curriculum. *Journal of Teaching in Physical Education*, 7, 265-288.

Macdonald, D., & Kirk, D. (1996). Private lives, public lives: Surveillance, identity and self in the work of beginning physical education teachers. *Sport, Education and Society*, 1(1), 59-75.

Macdonald, D., Kirk, D., & Braiuka, S. (1999). The social construction of the physical activity field at the school/university interface. *European Physical Education Review*, 5 (1), 31-51.

Macdonald, K. M. (1995). *The sociology of the professions*. London: Sage Publications. Mackreth, K. (1998). Developments in A level physical education. *The British Journal of Physical Education*, 29, 16-17.

Mann, M. (Ed.). (1983). *Macmillan student encyclopaedia of sociology*. London: Macmillan.

Mannheim, K. (1960). *Ideology and utopia: An introduction to the sociology of knowledge*. London: Routledge & Kegan Paul.

Mason, V. (1995). *Young people and sport in England, 1994: The views of teachers and children*. London: The Sports Council.

Mawer, M. (1996). *The effective teaching of physical education*. New York: Longman.

McCormack, A. (1997). Classroom management problems, strategies and influences in physical education. *European Physical Education Review*, 3(2), 102-115.

McGeorge, S. (1992). Results of the Allied Dunbar national fitness survey — impli-

References

cations for P.E. teachers. *Health and Physical Education Project Newsletter, 31,* 1-3.

McNamee, M. (1998). Philosophy and physical education: Analysis, epistemology and axiology. *European Physical Education Review,* 4(1), 75-91.

Mennell, S., & Goudsblom, J. (1998). *Norbert Elias: On civilization, power and knowledge.* Chicago: The University of Chicago Press.

Munrow, D. (1972). *Physical education: A discussion of principles.* London: Bell & Hyman.

Murdoch, E. (1992). Physical education today. *Bulletin of Physical Education, 28*(2), 15-24.

Murphy, P., Sheard, K., & Waddington, I. (2000). Figurational sociology and its application to sport. In J. Coakley & E. Dunning (Eds.), *Handbook of Sports Studies* (pp. 92-105). London: Sage.

Oakeshott, M. (1972). Education: The engagement and its frustration. In Robert Dearden, Paul Hirst & Richard Peters (Eds.), *Education and the development of reason. Part I. A critique of current educational aims* (pp. 17-47). London: Routledge & Kegan Paul.

O'Bryant, C. P., O'Sullivan, M., & Raudensky, J. (2000). Socialization of prospective physical education teachers: The story of new blood. *Sport, Education and Society, 5*(2), 177-193.

O'Donnell, M. (1981). *A new introduction to sociology.* London: Harrap.

Office for National Statistics (ONS) (1999). *Living in Britain: Results from the 1998 General Household Survey.* London: The Stationery Office.

Office for Standards in Education (OFSTED) (1998). *Secondary education 1993-97: The curriculum.* www.opengov.gov.uk.

O'Hear, A. (1981). *Education, society and human nature: An introduction to the philosophy of education.* London: Routledge & Kegan Paul.

Outhwaite, W. (1983). Knowledge, sociology of. In M. Mann (Ed.), *The Macmillan student encyclopaedia of sociology* (pp. 185-186). London: Macmillan.

Park, R. J. (1994). A decade of the body: Researching and writing about the history of health, fitness, exercise and sport, 1983-1993. *Journal of Sport History, 21*(1), 59-82.

Parry, J. (1988). Physical education, justification and the National Curriculum. *Physical Education Review, 11*(2), 106-118.

Parry, J. (1998). Reid on knowledge and justification in physical education. *European Physical Education Review,* 4(1), 70-74.

Penney, D. (1998). Positioning and defining physical education, sport and health in the curriculum. *European Physical Education Review,* 4(2), 117-126.

Penney, D., Clarke, G., & Kinchin, G. (2002). Developing physical education as a connective specialism: Is sport education the answer? *Sport, Education and Society, 7*(1), 55-64.

Penney, D., & Evans, J. (1997). Naming the game. Discourse and domination in physical education and sport in England and Wales. *European Physical Education Review, 3*(1), 21-32.

Penney, D., & Evans, J. (1998). Dictating the play: Government direction in physical education and sports policy development in England and Wales. In K. Green & K. Hardman (Eds.), *Physical education: A reader* (pp. 84-101). Aachen: Meyer & Meyer Verlag.

Penney, D., & Evans, J. (1999). *Politics, policy and practice in physical education.*

London: E. & F. N. Spon.

Penney, D., & Harris, D. (1997). Extra-curricular physical education: More of the same for the more able. *Sport, Education and Society, 2*(1), 41-54.

Placek, J. H., Dodds, P., Doolittle, S. A., Portman, P. A., Ratliffe, T. A., & Pinkham, K. M. (1995). Teaching recruits' physical education backgrounds and beliefs about purposes for their subject matter. *Journal of Teaching in Physical Education,14*, 246-261.

Prain, V., & Hickey, C. (1995). Using discourse analysis to change physical education. *QUEST, 47*, 76-90.

Qualifications and Curriculum Authority (QCA) (1999). *The review of the National Curriculum in England: The Secretary of State's proposals*. London: QCA.

Reid, A. (1996a). The concept of physical education in current curriculum and assessment policy in Scotland. *European Physical Education Review, 2*(1), 7-18.

Reid, A. (1996b). Knowledge, practice and theory in physical education. *European Physical Education Review, 2*(2), 94-104.

Reid, A. (1997). Value pluralism and physical education. *European Physical Education Review, 3*(1), 6-20.

Reid, A. (1999). Folk psychology, neuroscience and explanation in physical education. *European Physical Education Review, 5*(2), 101-120.

Roberts, K. (1995). School children and sport. In L. Lawrence, E. Murdoch & S. Parker (Eds.), *Professional and Development Issues in Leisure, Sport and Education* (Publication No. 56, pp. 337-348). Brighton: Leisure Studies Association.

Roberts, K. (1996a). Young people, schools, sport and government policy. *Sport, Education and Society, 1*(1), 47-57.

Roberts, K. (1996b). Youth cultures and sport: The success of school and community sports provisions in Britain. *European Physical Education Review, 2*(2), 105-115.

Roberts, K. (1997). Same activities, different meanings: British youth cultures in the 1990s. *Leisure Studies, 16*(1), 1-16.

Roberts, K., & Brodie, D. (1992). *Inner-city sport: Who plays and what are the benefits?* Culemborg: Giordano Bruno.

Schempp, P. G. (1989). Apprenticeship-of-observation and the development of physical education teachers. In T. J. Templin & P. G. Schempp (Eds.), *Socialisation into physical education: Learning to teach* (pp. 13-37). Indianapolis: Benchmark Press.

Scotson, J., & Elias, N. (1994). *The established and the outsiders: A sociological enquiry into community problems*. London: Sage Publications.

Scraton, S. (1992). *Shaping up to womanhood: Gender and girls' physical education*. Buckingham: Open University Press.

Scraton, S. (1995). Boys muscle in where angels fear to tread: Girls' sub-cultures and physical activity. In C. Critcher, P. Bramham & A. Tomlinson (Eds.), *Sociology of leisure: A reader* (pp. 117-129). London, E. & F. N. Spon.

Siedentop, D. (1994). *Sport education*. Champaign, IL: Human Kinetics.

Sparkes, A. C. (1990). Winners, losers and the myth of rational change in physical education: Towards an understanding of interests and power in innovation. In D. Kirk & R. Tinning (Eds.), *Physical education, curriculum and culture: Critical issues in the contemporary crisis* (pp. 193-224). London: The Falmer Press.

Sport England (2001). *Young people and sport in England 1999: A survey of young*

References

people and PE teachers. London: Sport England.

Sports Council for Wales (SCW) (1995). *The pattern of play: Physical education in Welsh secondary schools: 1990 to 1994*. Cardiff: SCW.

Swaan, A. de (2001). *Human societies: An Introduction*. Cambridge: Polity Press.

Talbot, M. (1995a). The politics of sport and physical education. In S. Fleming, M. Talbot & A. Tomlinson (Eds.), *Policy and politics in sport, physical education and leisure: Themes and issues* (Publication No. 55, pp. 3-26). Brighton: Leisure Studies Association.

Talbot, M. (1995b, July). Physical education and the National Curriculum: Some political issues. *Leisure Studies Association Newsletter, 41*, 20-30.

Templin, T. J., & Schempp, P. G. (1989). Socialization into physical education: Its heritage and hope. In T. J. Templin & P. G. Schempp (Eds.), *Socialization into physical education: Learning to teach* (pp. 1-11). Indianapolis: Benchmark Press.

Tinning, R. (1991). Problem-setting and ideology in health based physical education: An Australian perspective. *Physical Education Review, 14*(1), 40-49.

Tsangaridou, N., & Siedentop, D. (1995). Reflective teaching. A literature review. *QUEST, 14*, 212-237.

Underwood, G., Bird, S., & Farmiloe, H. (1993). Pupils' knowledge and understanding of health-related fitness in secondary schools. *The Bulletin of Physical Education, 29*(3), 47-63.

van Krieken, R. (1998). *Norbert Elias*. London: Routledge.

Waddington, I. (1975). The development of medical ethics: A sociological analysis. *Medical History, 19*, 36-51.

Waddington, I., Malcom, D., & Cobb, J. (1998). Gender stereotyping and physical education. *European Physical Education Review, 4*(1), 34-46.

Waddington, I., & Murphy P. (1992). Drugs, sport and ideologies. In E. Dunning & C. Rojek (Eds.), *Sport and leisure in the civilizing process* (pp. 36-64). London: Routledge.

Waring, M., & Almond, L. (1995). Games-centred games: A revolutionary or evolutionary alternative for games teaching. *European Physical Education Review, 1*(1), 55-66.

Weber, M. (1949). Objectivity in social science and social policy. In E. Shils & H. Finch (Eds.), *The methodology of the social sciences* (pp. 68-103). New York: Free Press.

Williams, A. (1988). The historiography of health and fitness in physical education. *British Journal of Physical Education Research Supplement, 3*, 1-4.

Wilterdink, N. A. (1977). Norbert Elias's sociology of knowledge and its significance for the study of the sciences. In P. R. Gleichmann, J. Goudsblom & H. Korte (Eds.), *Human figurations: Essays for Norbert Elias* (pp. 110-126). Amsterdam: Stichting Amsterdams Sociologisch Tijdschrift.

Wirth, L. (1960). Preface. In Karl Mannheim, *Ideology and utopia* (pp. xiii-xxxi). London: Routledge & Kegan Paul.

Index

Prepared by John Cubitt, PhD, Member of the Society of Indexers

The index covers all materials in the book, except the preface, contents and references. Index entries are arranged alphabetically in word-by-word order with entries referring to page numbers. Subheadings are in set-out style according to BS ISO 999: 1996 and BS 1749: 1985. Note that the terms chosen for index entries are those that are generally utilised within this book, but may vary from local alternatives or language spellings.

Index